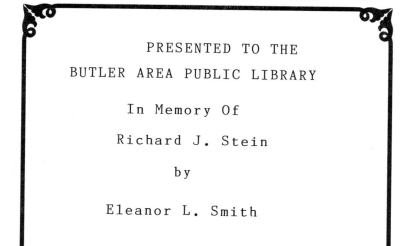

THE FOUNDATIONS OF BETTER
WOODWORKING

BY

JEFF MILLER

POPULAR WOODWORKING BOOKS
CINCINNATI, OHIO
www.popularwoodworking.com

TABLE OF CONTENTS

PREFACE

Over the course of a long teaching career, I have found that a large number of students – even the most thoughtful and well-equipped – lack the most fundamental level of knowledge and skills. It's no mystery that this core knowledge is missing; most of the woodworking literature and other woodworking media pays little attention to these fundamentals. Instead, the usual preference is to dive directly into a project or the specific techniques needed to handle some element of a project. Some articles and books cover methods of work, but still tend to omit the basic principles of wood, tools and body mechanics that need to be understood before one can successfully cut to a line, plane a surface flat and smooth, or fit a joint properly.

If a solid foundation of basic skills and knowledge is lacking, a woodworker will never perfect the techniques that he or she needs to advance. For example, it's rarely a lack of information on how to cut dovetails that keeps most woodworkers from being able to cut the joint successfully. It's the lack of basic sawing skills, the inability to cut to a line properly, or the failure to wield a chisel effectively. These skills themselves are based on proper body position and mechanics, a fundamental understanding of the properties of wood, the knowledge of how the tools actually work and an understanding of just what it means to cut to a line.

Body position and biomechanics are the source of both the force and the control needed to use both the saw and the chisel properly. The knowledge of wood's structure, in combination with an understanding of how these tools actually cut through wood, supply more vital information about how the tools should be used. And it all comes together when the woodworker understands just where in relationship to a marked line the wood needs to be removed. And of course, there's the element of practice. But knowing exactly what you're trying to accomplish when you practice is essential to your ability to get there. Without these fundamentals, no description of the steps involved in cutting the joint will make a difference in the ability to get the job done.

My own background is as a professional musician, both as a performer and as a teacher. It came as a great surprise to me that so many woodworkers didn't take a more systematic approach as they learned their craft. Musicians most often begin with basics of how to use the body properly for their instrument (or even more directly, for their voice). Hand position, posture and even breathing all play an important role. The foundation of music itself is studied as well; one learns about the underlying tonal and formal structure. And finally, music history rounds out the education; one learns not only about what music happened when, but also the nuances of style that go along with different types of music.

Musicians hear more in the music than casual listeners. Likewise, true craftsmen see more in both the wood and in the overall form, structure and details of a piece of furniture than the casual woodworker. This is the result of training, of either the ear or the eye.

Similar concepts apply to most athletic endeavors. Whether swinging a golf club or a tennis racket, running, cycling or swimming, the mechanics of how you use your body and how well you understand the specific demands of the sport and the equipment will have an enormous impact on how well you are able to perform.

Musicians and athletes have established methods for developing better fundamentals, and there are many different types of training resources that emphasize these essential basics.

Woodworkers, in contrast, tend to get some tools, pick a project, and jump in. Some are able to succeed this way. An astute student will pick up some of the core knowledge through trial and error, or through careful observation of others. Much more can be learned under the eye of a good instructor, who can point out fundamental problems and guide the student toward correct usage of tools and the materials. But if the student doesn't begin to understand the basics, even this is not enough.

A traditional apprenticeship program provided much of the structure found in learning music or in athletic training. It not only taught the fundamentals, but also provided exposure to the master's high-level work. This made it absolutely clear what the end results needed to be. The apprentice slowly worked his way up from the simplest of tasks to the more complex, all directly under the supervision of the master and the higher-level workers in the shop.

My goal for this book is to create a significant resource for woodworkers – to pull together as much of the fundamental woodworking knowledge as possible so it can be easily learned and then applied in a wide variety of woodworking situations. It can't quite be the equivalent of an apprenticeship, or working directly under a great teacher, but it should provide a more comprehensive understanding of the essentials of woodworking than is currently available with other resources.

My point is not to show you how to do everything. In fact, someone showing you how to do something doesn't mean that you're going to be able to do it at all. Instead, my goal is to provide a foundation of understanding upon which all woodworking skills can be built and improved.

INTRODUCTION

The content of this book might best be described with an analogy. Let's say you want to drive from your house to a friend's new house in another state. To drive there you will need a number of things, many of which you might take for granted. First, you'll need a car and the ability to drive that car. Also assumed is the knowledge of how a car works, the basics of driving on a system of roads and the various rules of the road. You'll need a map (digital or otherwise), and you'll need to know the precise location of your destination. You also need some sort of feedback mechanism active the entire time you're driving, not only to keep you on your correct course, but also to keep your car on the road, traveling at an appropriate speed, and reacting to the vagaries of the traffic, road and weather conditions around you.

Most woodworkers are absolutely delighted by the "car." And there are an awful lot of "maps" out there. But what about the exact destination, and how to actually drive the car and keep everything on course – despite all of the usual and unforeseen variables one might encounter? These discussions are pretty rare. What do I mean by an exact destination? Much as you need a precise street address to get to a specific house when driving, in your woodworking you need to be able to envision precisely what you're trying to do.

Another analogy might be useful here. In music, it's not enough to just know what notes you're supposed to play. You have to get the pitch and the volume right, and play that note at exactly the right time. You have to balance these things with other musicians who may also be playing. There's more. In order for the music to make sense, you need to understand how each note fits into the melody and the harmony so that the music makes sense. And then you can start to shape musical phrases and express the musical ideas.

I recall one notorious high school band rehearsal, where our band director, a very talented musician, was trying to convey all of this to us. Although this was almost 40 years ago, it made an enormous impact on everyone in the band. For the entire hour-long rehearsal we played only the first few measures of the piece we were working on – a total of about three seconds of music. Absolutely everything was pointed out, balanced, adjusted and perfected. And throughout the rehearsal, more and more people started to understand what the director and the music demanded of us.

This is no less true in woodworking. You want to dovetail a drawer well. That means not only knowing how to lay out and cut the joint, but how tightly the joint should fit, how close to your scribed line you have to cut to get that fit, and how to use all of your tools to get you to that exact place with clean, perpendicular edges and straight lines. And that just amounts to the basics of getting the joint right. The appearance of the joint (angle, spacing, size of pins, wood choice, edge and corner treatment, degree of finish…) also has to fit in with the rest of the piece.

This brings up a crucial part of the idea of destination: having a clear understanding of the quality of the work you're trying to do. This is a matter of choice, and is not an inflexible standard. The hope is that your standards will increase as you learn, and you become better able to both see, understand and do quality work. Most of the time you'll strive for the very highest level you can imagine, but in places – sometimes even on the same job – those standards may be relaxed a little. This was true even in some of the finest of period furniture; hidden away from sight, the work was purely functional. Some jobs may call for different

If you don't know where you're going, there is remarkably little chance you're going to get there.

standards altogether. In any case, you need to set out with certain standards of quality in mind, and then work to hold to those standards.

You're not going to get better just because you've got a better sense of quality. But you won't get better without that sense of quality. You need that sense of where you're going to be able to work on all of the steps to get you there.

Some of the increased awareness of quality is amazingly easy to acquire. On a basic level, if you don't know about machine marks, cross-grain scratches or the way sanding can round over or blur a surface, will you even see these things? It's unlikely. But once you've been made aware, they will be glaringly obvious. How is a tenon supposed to fit its mortise? If you don't know exactly how it's supposed to look and feel, why it has to fit that way, and the various problems that might befall you as you try to make the joint, how will you manage to make one fit properly?

So how do we set out to fill in this missing woodworking knowledge? How do we build this foundation of understanding?

We'll work first on understanding the basic information that applies to our material and our tools – in terms of our analogy, we'll be talking about the "car" and the road system.

The best way to improve our understanding here is to come up with appropriate mental models for how these things work. In terms of our analogy, we'll form a picture (simplified, but accurate) of how the road systems and the car actually work, so we're not relying on incorrect assumptions (the car is powered by hamsters running on exercise wheels under the hood, for example). Then we'll move on to the driving – using your body properly to drive the car, and learning to see and to observe what's going on around you more accurately. We'll learn more about staying on course, and how to get better at all of the necessary driving skills.

And finally, we'll cover some very practical methods for improving: how to deal with mistakes; learning to get more feedback as you work; and how to experiment with and practice your skills.

My hope is that at the end of this, you'll not only be a better woodworker, but you'll have a foundation upon which you can improve much further.

Pay Attention

There is very little mindless work in woodworking. First of all, your safety depends on always paying attention to what's going on, no matter how repetitious the task. In fact, you need to pay extra attention to safety in situations where you naturally tend to let your mind wander. But just as important is paying attention to quality throughout your work, and to improving each and every task you perform over the course of a project.

SECTION ONE:

UNDERSTANDING

THE BASICS

CHAPTER ONE

My son, Isaac, helps out with new way of sizing lumber in my shop. The board breaks along the grain lines.

UNDERSTANDING THE WOOD

Working with wood can be extraordinarily rewarding. When all goes well, your work can produce sensuously smooth furniture that begs to be touched, glows with a natural warmth, and that, with care, can last for centuries. But wood can also be a source of incredible frustration as pieces crack, warp, twist, expand, contract, and joints fail. Although wood occasionally does behave as if it were intentionally creating mischief, most often, the problems come from a lack of knowledge of the material. Wood is not a stable, inert material. It gains and loses moisture, reacts to temperature, and ages over time. Rarely can you take it for granted. But the more you know about wood's structure and how that structure defines its properties, the more you'll be able to deal with almost all of the difficulties it can cause.

The Big Bundle of Straws

The single-most important thing to understand about wood is that it is not a homogeneous material, and it doesn't behave like one. If you cut it in one direction you've got one set of properties. Turn it around and it's as if you've got a different material in your hands. Rotate it 90°, and you've got something else entirely. Wood has distinctly different sets of properties when worked on in each of four orientations: with the grain, against the grain, across the grain and across end grain. And on some boards, you don't even have to rotate the wood; you'll find all of these different properties within inches on the same surface.

Why is this? Wood is fibrous. The best way to picture it is as a giant bundle of loosely connected straws. When wood is part of a living tree, some of the fibers act as straws, drinking up water and minerals from the soil and transporting them to the crown of the tree. Other fibers carry sugars from the leaves back through the tree to the various growing cells.

Of course, this is an over-simplification. However, this basic mental image is enough to tell you an awful lot about how wood behaves, and it can help you to work more successfully with wood.

Let's start with one of the most important properties of our bundle of straws. Although the straws themselves can certainly break, they are significantly stronger than the connections between them. In other words, individual wood fibers are stronger than the bond between them. This is very important in understanding many different characteristics of wood. Most obviously, a board will be

Fig. 1-1 - This is a different kind of "board breaking," and one that is much more useful. The log has been split into wedge-shaped boards.

much stronger if the fibers run along its length than if they run across its width.

Working with Wood

Knock a wedge into the end of a log or parallel to the fibers and it will split along the fibers. Follow this process to create a rough board, and you'll wind up with a piece of wood whose fibers run in exactly the same direction as the edges of the board, and therefore gives you a very strong board (Fig. 1-1).

You might think that this would be common knowledge, and incredibly useful knowledge at that. But these days, only a few shops that specialize in chairs, period furniture or steam bending do much splitting of lumber. The vast

Board Breaking

On a large scale, a good demonstration of wood's greater strength along its fibers is unrelated to woodworking. Various martial arts require one to break boards as a test of strength and accuracy (see photo, p. 10). Breaking a board where the fibers run along the length of the board (held at the ends) is very difficult indeed. But board breaking in martial arts is done with boards that have the fibers running the short way across the board (in other words, it's held at the sides). It still takes good aim and a sharp blow to break the board, but it snaps between the fibers surprisingly easily.

majority of boards that are available have been sawn out of a log. Wood fibers in sawn boards rarely line up perfectly parallel to an edge.

Fibers don't necessarily grow straight either. Wood fibers can curve, twist and head off in all directions, based on how the tree grew. This can make splitting the wood pretty much impossible, and is certainly one reason that sawing wood is the norm. Sawmills cut the boards along the length of the tree, but that doesn't guarantee that the fibers will run in that direction. Trees are not simple cylinders either. Even the straightest trees are fatter at the bottom and taper toward the top. They also grow in response to their environment, which is constantly changing.

There are many instances in woodworking where you might end up with a board that has fibers running the 'wrong' way, across the board. This is most common if you cut out a shape that has curves. Whatever the cause, if the fibers go across a board the short way, it is called short grain, which creates a point of weakness you need to be aware of. Plenty of woodworkers seem to feel that wood is generally strong enough to ignore these problems. But the fact that some people don't pay attention to fiber direction doesn't mean it's not important. You'll do much better if you watch out for it and take it into account.

Woodworkers use plenty of tools besides wedges, although most of these tools are, in essence, very sharp wedges. The wedging action and the fibrous nature of wood play an important role in how tools actually work. The exaggerated model of how this works – the bundle of straws – can help clarify this interaction.

As mentioned above, the fibers in wood don't necessarily grow straight, and the board that's cut from the tree only rarely has fibers that run straight from end to end. So a better model for the bundle of straws would include this information: The straws may angle up toward the surface, or curve this way and that. It's not hard to imagine what might happen if you try to slice into the bundle with a cutting edge. If the straws angle up toward the edge, it is likely that the edge will catch on the straws and pry them up rather than slice them cleanly; it takes less force to wedge them apart from their neighbors than it does to cut them. (Fig. 1-2).

On the other hand, if the straws emerge from the surface angled away from the cutting edge, the edge can slice through them. There's nothing for the cutting edge to catch on or wedge apart. In addition, the straws that are behind and beneath the surface support those at the surface, and the cutting edge can sever them cleanly (Fig. 1-3).

Cuts that go across the bundle (on the surface, and perpendicular to the length of the fibers) will separate straws more than slice them. Imagine peeling up a layer of them (Fig. 1-4). Unless the cut happens to be the full

Fig. 1-2 - Paring with a chisel against the direction of the fibers, the wood splits out ahead of and below the intended cut.

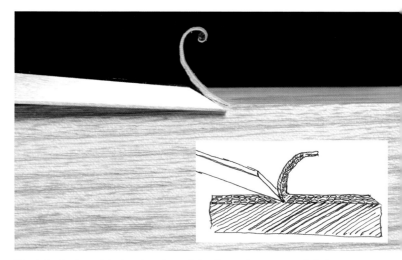

Fig. 1-3 - Paring with the direction of the fibers does not split below the intended cut.

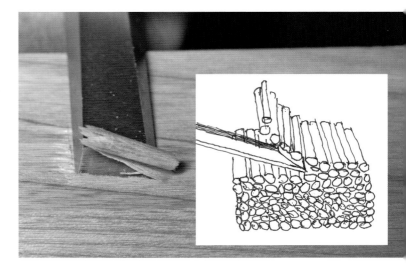

Fig. 1-4 - Notice how the fibers break off beyond the sides of the cut when you pare across the fibers.

width of the bundle, the cut will have ragged edges. The straws will likely break off beyond the tool at either end, At the far end of the bundle, the straws may break off rather significantly.

When you cut across the grain on a piece of wood, the shavings have a very different look and feel from those cut with the grain. You can imagine them as a pile of connected miniature straws. And they feel different, too. They are sharp and surprisingly irritating if they get down your shirt (Fig. 1-5).

You might have to score a piece of wood to sever the fibers before attempting to plane or chisel across the grain. There are also some highly specific rabbeting planes designed for cutting across the grain, which incorporate an additional cutting edge (a nicker) to score the wood fibers at the edge of the cut.

There are still other issues that come up when cutting across the end of a board. The bundle of straws also helps explain these. Starting the cut won't pose a problem; the bulk of the bundle backs up the initial part of the cut. As you reach the far side of the bundle, however, there are fewer and fewer straws backing up the ones you are attempting to cut. A point will finally come where the force needed to push the cutting edge through the straws is greater than the adhesive force holding the straws on the back of the bundle together. The result is predictable:

Fig. 1-5 - You get a real sense of the fibers when you plane across the grain. Notice that the back edge of the board is splitting off (spelching) as well.

Fig. 1-6 - Planing end-grain will split the unsupported fibers at the far edge of the board.

Fig. 1-7 - Chop too aggressively with a chisel and you'll have a mess like this, too.

Straws will simply split off and break as you get to the far end of the bundle. And fibers do indeed break off as you get to the far edge of a board. (Fig. 1-6)

The straws in the bundle (and fibers in a board) also compress a little as the edge of a tool starts to cut. This is actually true on all cuts, but is most obvious on the end of the bundle. Even with the sharpest of edges, the straws will compress a little bit before the tool starts to cut through; there needs to be enough force pushing back against the edge of the cutting tool for it to be able to cut. A larger wedge angle, a duller edge, or a cut that is too fast may compress the straws even more before they actually cut, and may completely separate straws from their neighbors before any cutting happens. This makes for a much rougher cut. If you try to cut even harder, the straws may simply break off below the surface instead of cutting. (Fig. 1-7)

It's not uncommon when dealing with wood to find boards with fibers that seem to wander all over the place. The fibers emerge on the surface of the board in one di-rection in one spot, and emerge in a different direction just a short distance away. This can be very frustrating, and it becomes difficult to avoid tear-out. In general, the solution is to use a steeper cutting angle. The higher angle does not wedge up fibers as easily. And depending on the angle, the wood is subject to a different cutting action; in-stead of the slicing action of a lower angle, the high angle will cause compression failure and then a smashing off of the fibers. This is less likely to tear up fibers, but does not leave as good a surface as one you've successfully planed clean. There are more specific recommendations in the chapter on using your tools.

Gluing Wood Together

The fibrous nature of wood also is important when con-sidering how to glue pieces together. The straw analogy continues to be helpful in explaining this. In order to glue together bundles of straws successfully, the long sides of the straws must be glued together. They don't need to be parallel – angles are fine – but sides of the straws must be

Planing Across End Grain

One way to deal with the real-world issue of separating fibers when planing end grain is to moisten the end of the board just before cutting (water and mineral spirits, both work, but mineral spirits will evaporate off quicker, and won't rust your tools). This will swell up the fibers enough to cut down on the compression, and usually allows for a cleaner cut. Of course, a very sharp blade and a more acute cutting angle help as well.

Fig. 1-8 - Only a few fibers actually adhered to the end-grain in this long-grain-to-end-grain glue joint. The joint failed right at the glue line.

Fig. 1-9 - This long-grain-to-long-grain joint broke next to the glue line, but not on it.

glued to other sides. It's easy to imagine that gluing the ends of the straws will lead to problems. There's less actual surface there, and the straws will actually soak up most of the glue. A glue joint on the end of the bundle won't form a strong connection to anything else.

That's not as obvious with wood, but it's no less true. We'll certainly be able to get end grain to stick to something (even other end grain), but it won't hold well, and will break apart under stress or shock (Fig. 1-8). None of the end-grain fibers will attach to other fibers, and the joint will break apart right at the glue line.

Glue bonds that are from fiber to fiber are generally stronger than the wood itself. In other words, good glue bonds tend to be stronger than the bonds that naturally occur between the fibers. This is true with just about any wood glue. Breaking apart a good fiber-to-fiber joint (a long-grain-to-long-grain joint) you'll almost always break apart the wood next to the joint, not the joint itself. (Fig. 1-9)

Beyond the Bundle of Straws

There are a few properties of wood that the bundle of straws model can't explain fully. In order to understand these properties of wood, we need to elaborate a little bit on our simple model of how wood works.

A tree is constantly adding new fibrous cells just underneath the bark. This new wood accumulates at different rates based on growing conditions. There is quicker growth and larger and thicker-walled cells during moderate and wetter months with more available nutrients, and slower growth with smaller and thinner-walled cells during dryer, hotter months. It's worth noting that in tropical

conditions, where the difference in seasons is minimal or subtle, the cell growth is much more consistent. Annual climate conditions will also have an effect, with drier years (or multi-year periods) showing less overall growth than wetter ones.

The difference between these growth periods is variously called earlywood and latewood, or springwood and summerwood, and in most of the woods we're familiar with, is noticeably different in either density, porosity and/or color. This is the difference we saw in the growth rings we counted on a tree stump as children. These are called annual rings if the growth pattern changes annually. And it is the difference between these layers that is a major factor in the grain patterns that we see in wood.

What we typically think of as wood grain is the result of slicing a board out of a tree, and cutting across these growth rings in various ways. Different ways of cutting the board out of the log result in very different appearances, and somewhat different structural characteristics as well. The fact that a tree is not cylindrical, but is instead somewhat conical, also affects the patterns created from cutting wood from the tree.

Heartwood and Sapwood

After a certain number of years have added more and more outer layers, the now-inner layers transition from being active transporters of nutrients to more of a structural role in the tree. This defines the difference between sapwood (the active transport component near the bark) and heartwood (the inner, structural wood), which often have different colors both in the tree and in the wood. While this difference is functionally significant in the tree,

Plain-sawn or Flat-sawn, Quartersawn and Rift-sawn Wood

Wood is most often plain-sawn (or flat-sawn, the terms are interchangeable). The appearance of the surface is generally characterized by arches, vees and ellipses in the grain patterns. The ends of the boards will usually show the curvature of the tree's annual rings.

Wood can also be quartersawn. This term comes for the practice of first cutting the log into quarters, and then sawing each quarter into boards. The alignment of the annual rings tend to be perpendicular to the surfaces. The surfaces usually display straight grain, with some additional figure (see below).

Rift-sawn grain (a less-precise term) covers wood with the annual rings oriented somewhere between 45° to 90° to the surface. This displays straight grain on the surfaces, but usually without the additional figure. When the growth rings are at roughly

45° to the surface, the wood is idea for table and chair legs, because it will display the same basic grain pattern on all four sides. Note that a flat-sawn board will have edges that show quartersawn grain, and vice versa.

Here are two possible cutting patterns for getting mostly flat-sawn boards out of a log. Note that when cutting up a round log into flat boards, not all of the boards will have the same grain orientation.

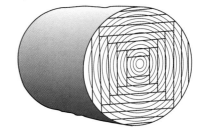

Typical flat-sawn grain pattern

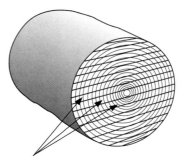

These boards will be quartersawn

Typical quarter-sawn grain pattern

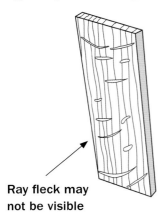

Ray fleck may not be visible

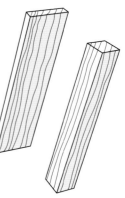

Typical rift-sawn grain pattern

Two possible cutting patterns for quartersawn and rift-sawn boards. Both patterns yield some of each type of grain.

Fig. 1-10 - Cherry, poplar and walnut all display the difference between sapwood and heartwood with different colors.

Fig. 1-11 - Quartersawn white oak (right) shows more ray-fleck that the quartersawn walnut (at left).

and can result in very different relative moisture levels between heartwood and sapwood in a freshly cut board, by the time the board is dried, the differences are mostly cosmetic. (Fig. 1-10)

Radial Cells and Their Effects

All of the cells in a tree don't run up and down the trunk. There are important cells that radiate out from the center, providing lateral transfer of nutrients and water. The prominence and size of these radial cells vary from species to species, and can be almost invisible or a defining characteristic of certain quartersawn boards. The radial cells also have an effect on the wood, changing its behavior, as we'll see in the next section. (Fig. 1-11)

Wood Movement

Wood responds in significant ways to changes in its moisture content. And the moisture content of the wood is affected by the changes in the moisture content of the air around it. The wood is constantly releasing or absorbing moisture from the air as it seeks to establish equilibrium. This is a fundamental property of wood, and one that has a major impact on many aspects of woodworking.

When freshly cut from a log, a typical hardwood board can have a relative moisture content (defined as the relation between the weight of the board as freshly cut to its weight completely dried out in an oven) of somewhere between 60 and 100 percent. For most woodworking, the wood is dried to somewhere around 6 to 15 percent. This

can happen either by letting it sit exposed to the air for a significant amount of time, which usually results in a in 10 to 15 percent relative moisture content (depending on the climate), or by placing it in a special kiln that will, through a combination of heat and dehumidification, remove moisture in a carefully controlled way, usually down to 6 to 8 percent.

Our more complete bundle of straws model can help us understand how this change in moisture affects the wood. The straws are, for the most part, tubular cell structures. These cellular structures shrink down as the cell walls dry out, but are capable of swelling back up when they regain moisture. They do not lengthen appreciably with added moisture, but they do get fatter. A substantial amount of this movement is confined by the radial cells – the cells that extend outward from the center of the tree. It's as if these cells tie our bundle together a little tighter between the growth rings. That means that most of the swelling of cells is directed perpendicular to those radial cells, or tangent to the growth rings. In other words, the straws become more oval in cross section as they dry out. The overall effect is that the bundle changes dimension the most in this tangential direction, less so radially and hardly at all lengthwise.

The difference in the amount of change in different directions is a major factor in woodworking. Most furniture isn't made from wood that's all aligned the same way; it's made from many pieces of wood oriented in different ways. The fibers in the aprons of a table run horizontally between the legs, whose fibers run vertically. The top is in a dif-

Wood Movement Issues to Watch For

The most common problems caused by wood movement came from confining wood movement. You have to let the wood move. Wood that can't expand and contract will inevitably cause trouble. The force behind this expansion and contraction is stronger than the wood itself. Cracks, blown-apart frames, split tabletops, and more are almost always the result of not making allowances for the wood to move with seasonal changes in humidity.

Try to limit cross-grain joinery to 3" or less. This is a fairly safe joint size, and larger cross-grain joints are prone to breaking apart or cracking due to constrained cross-grain movement.

There is some movement in all joints that have grain at right angles, but most wood glues are designed with enough flexibility to accommodate small amounts of movement. Over the course of decades, most glues will fail due to this differential movement. You should consider grain orientation in your joints, if possible, as a way of minimizing this movement.

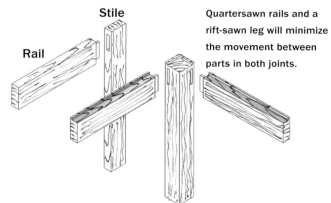

Quartersawn rails and stiles mean minimal change in the width of the rail tenons and minimal change to the depths of the mortises.

Stile

Rail

Quartersawn rails and a rift-sawn leg will minimize the movement between parts in both joints.

In joints between panels (dovetails, finger joints, sliding dovetails, etc.) the grain should be similar on both parts. Flat-sawn-to-flat-sawn, or quartersawn-to-quartersawn.

Don't glue up a panel with quartersawn grain and flatsawn grain right next to one-another – the difference in the direction of movement from one piece to the next will show up as a ridge between the boards once they start to move; ultimately, this disparity will work to destroy this glue joint as well.

ferent plane from any of the other pieces. All of these pieces expand and contract in certain dimensions, but not in others. And we want the table to stay together despite this. (Fig. 1-12)

The expansion and contraction of wood is the major reason wood gives us so much trouble – at least in environments where there is a great deal of seasonal change in moisture content. In fairly constant climates (the desert, the tropics or other similar areas with little seasonal moisture change) wood movement just isn't a big factor. The moisture content of the air is almost always the same, and the wood (once it has acclimated to this humidity level) remains mostly the same as well. At least it does until the wood or the furniture is moved somewhere else.

But there are also other vexing problems with wood movement: Wood warps in various ways, and checks and cracks. Some of these problems are hard to avoid. But most of the time it comes back to a lack of awareness of how wood naturally behaves.

Why does wood move in these ways? There are a few factors involved, but most of the time

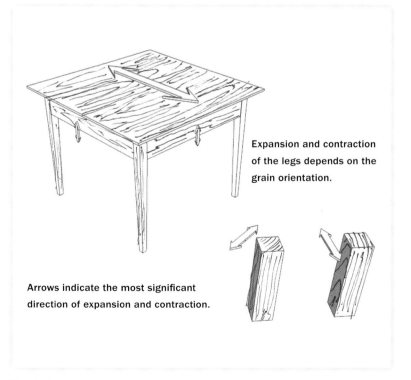

Expansion and contraction of the legs depends on the grain orientation.

Arrows indicate the most significant direction of expansion and contraction.

Fig. 1-12

Warping Wood

There are four descriptive terms that cover the various misbehaviors known collectively as warping (and plenty of other non-sanctioned words that might come to mind as well). These are cup, bow, crook and twist. Each defines a particular kind of wood movement. Sadly, they are not mutually exclusive. That's where some additional not-officially-sanctioned words come into play.

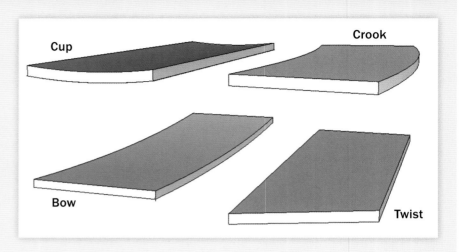

it comes back to the issue of moisture.

Any time the moisture content on one surface of a board is different from that on the other side, one side will expand or contract more than the other side. And that differential movement causes the board to cup. This happens in many different situations, some of them less than obvious.

How do you wind up with one side of the board wetter than the other side (other than actually wetting the board on one side)? One common way for this to happen is to finish one side of a board, but not the other. It can also happen if the two sides are finished differently. Finishes provide some protection for the wood, and also slow down (but only rarely eliminate) the exchange of moisture with the surrounding air. If the finish isn't balanced on both sides, when the atmospheric moisture content changes, one side will adjust more quickly than the other. This means that the fibers on one side will swell up or shrink down quicker than those on the other side. An unconstrained board may then warp.

Milling a board can also create a moisture imbalance if you're not careful. To understand this, let's examine more closely how wood dries. When freshly cut wood is placed either in a specialized kiln or out in the air, the wood immediately starts to lose moisture to the surrounding drier air as it seeks equilibrium with its environment. End grain loses moisture much faster than the sides of the fibers. Because of this, it is important to seal the ends of a board (a special paint, wax or other moisture-resistant finish is usually used), or the ends will shrink so much faster than the wood closer to the middle of the board that the ends will crack to accommodate the difference. When the ends are sealed, the bulk of the drying starts in the outer layers of the wood, and that in turn helps to pull moisture out of the inner layers.

Eventually, when equilibrium is reached, no further drying occurs. Any change in the environment, however, will cause either more moisture loss or moisture gain. Either way, the process starts on the outside of the board and moves in. If the wood does not reach a new equilibrium, there will be some imbalance between the inside and the outside of the wood. This is not necessarily a problem, and in fact, boards are in this state of flux much of the time in climates with significant swings in humidity. A board can go through this cycle over and over and not warp or cup.

If, however, one removes wood from one side of this board and not the other (or more from one side than the other), it is possible that the board will wind up in a situation where the moisture content of the two sides is not the same. One side will have the moisture content that was on

Glue-line Swelling

Water-based glues add a little bit of moisture to the wood around a joint, swelling the fibers up temporarily. This swelling subsides within a day or two as the small amount of moisture added to the wood dissipates. This is not normally an issue. However, if you glue up a panel and then smooth it before the moisture dissipates (this usually takes at least 24 hours), you may create a problem. Smoothing out the glue line when it is still swelled up means that when it dries back out, it will shrink down below the level of the rest of the panel. You'll see this as little valleys at each of the glue-lines. This will be most visible with glossy finishes, which tend to accentuate surface irregularities.

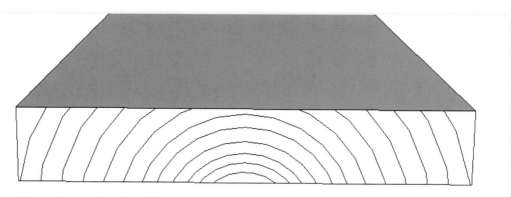

The top face has both flat-sawn grain (toward the middle) and rift-sawn (out at the edges), while the bottom surface has more quartered and rift grain. The top surface will move more than the bottom when the moisture changes.

Fig. 1-13

the outside of the board, and the other side will wind up with the moisture content from the core of the board. The wetter side will then shrink more than the drier one, causing cupping. You can avoid this problem by balancing the milling process, and milling wood equally from both sides.

You can also run into moisture differentials from the inside to the outside of a wooden case, such as a box or a cabinet that is tightly closed. Atmospheric moisture changes on the outside may affect the inside of the piece more slowly, and cause problems on wider, unrestrained panels. Allowing air to circulate inside the case will solve the problem. Most traditional designs evolved to deal with this issue; these will be covered at the end of the chapter.

If a board is dried too quickly, you can also wind up with a different problem arising from moisture imbalance. The board will crack and/or check. This happens when one part of the board dries out faster than another part. We've already seen that moisture migrates out of a board much faster through the ends than it does through the sides of the fibers. If nothing is done to control this natural tendency, the ends of the board will shrink much faster than the wood that is closer to the middle. In order to adapt to the contraction at the end of the board adjacent to wood that is still swollen with moisture, the end fibers may split apart. It's amazing that the shrinkage of the wood is so strong it will pull the board apart. Standard practice when drying wood calls for sealing the ends of the boards to eliminate (or at least slow down) the faster moisture loss and to allow the wood to dry out evenly.

Too rapid drying can still cause trouble even if the ends of the boards are sealed, however. The accelerated drying may cause the outer layers on the sides of the board to shrink too quickly for the moisture to migrate out from the inner layers. You may find cracks throughout the surfaces of the board as the wood deals with outer layers that have contracted around a core that is still moist and plump.

Growth Ring Orientation

Most wood (except some quartersawn wood) is cut from a tree so that we see the curvature of the growth rings in the end-grain. Wood that originated closer to the center of the tree will show more curvature (a tighter radius) than that cut closer to the bark. The more curvature, the more prone the board will be to cupping. This is not a moisture imbalance issue, but it is still moisture related. A board with pronounced curvature actually has significantly different grain orientation from one side to the other; the outside of the curve will show more movement along its surface, which is tangent to the curve. The inside of the curve has less movement along its face; the grain has changed enough that it behaves more like quartersawn wood and has more movement perpendicular to the face. The overall tendency then is for this board to cup as if the growth rings visible on end grain were trying to straighten out as the wood dries out, and to curve more as the board gains moisture. (Fig. 1-13)

There is another problem that can show up in a board that is cut too close to the center of the tree (the pith). The wood there actually has a somewhat different structure than wood cut from areas farther out in the tree, and it responds to losing and gaining moisture in notably different ways as well. This wood (known as juvenile wood) can cause serious warping in a board and should be avoided.

Environmental Factors

Trees don't always grow straight and tall. Their growth is influenced by what goes on around them in the surrounding forest, the terrain on which they grow, and the climate. At times, one (or several) of these factors can cause changes that affect the growth and resulting structure of the wood. In addition, physical stresses on a growing tree, such as consistently windy conditions, growing on a steep slope or with shifting soil, can also distort a tree significantly, creating a great deal of built-up stress in the wood. These trees may grow at an angle, or bend as they grow. Trees are also phototropic – they grow toward the light – and a tree will respond to changes in light due to a fallen or rapidly growing tree nearby. This, too, can cause

Make a Cutlist as the First Step Toward Understanding What You Should Be Doing With the Wood

One of the best things you can do as you start on a project is to make up your own cutlist. This is a perfect opportunity to consider all of the possibilities for grain choice. Sure, some projects come with a ready-made cut lists. But you do yourself a disservice by skipping this step and relying on someone else's idea of the project. Making your own cutlist is the best way to really get acquainted with the project you're about to build, and is especially important for making appropriate wood choices.

Making a cut list forces you to go through the project drawings and think about each piece and how it functions as part of the whole project. And this gives you an opportunity to think through exactly what wood (or wood grain) will suit that part best. This is the first step in your project toward doing a better job.

If you're simply interested in the efficiency of wood use, you can make choices based on that as well. But at least you'll be making your own choices. And you'll still have a better concept of the project, and a clearer idea of exactly where you're going.

Don't just make a list, either. Annotate that list with descriptions that will help you choose the best wood for each part of the job.

A SIMPLE TABLE WITH DRAWER

NUMBER	PART	THICKNESS X WIDTH X LENGTH	NOTES
4	legs	$1\frac{1}{2}$" x $1\frac{1}{2}$" x $23\frac{3}{4}$"	Rift-sawn grain (so the grain appears straight on all four sides). Mortised for side and back aprons, half-blind dovetail at top of leg for front upper stretcher, twin tenons for lower stretcher
3	aprons	$\frac{3}{4}$" x 4" x $13\frac{1}{2}$"	Quartersawn or rift-sawn grain, $\frac{3}{4}$"-long tenons on both ends (12" between the tenons)
1	upper stretcher	$\frac{3}{4}$" x $1\frac{1}{2}$" x 13"	Dovetailed at ends ($\frac{1}{2}$" long) to attach to top of legs (12" between dovetails)
1	lower stretcher	$\frac{3}{4}$" x $1\frac{1}{2}$" by $13\frac{1}{2}$"	Twin tenons at ends (oriented vertically for maximum long grain glue surface) – $\frac{3}{4}$" long (12" between tenons)
1	top	$\frac{3}{4}$" x 18" x 18"	Made up of three or four pieces cut from the same board. Match the grain with care. Boards should be the same width
1	drawer front	$\frac{3}{4}$" x $2\frac{1}{2}$" x 12"	Symmetrical grain. Look for something interesting. Half-blind dovetails. Stopped groove for drawer bottom
2	drawer sides	$\frac{1}{2}$" x $2\frac{1}{2}$" x $13\frac{15}{16}$"	Secondary wood – maple, even grain. Stopped grooves for drawer bottom
1	drawer back	$\frac{1}{2}$" x 2" x 12"	Secondary wood as for sides. One less dovetail than at the front of the drawer.

Drawer bottom $\frac{3}{8}$" x roughly $13\frac{3}{16}$" x $11\frac{1}{2}$" Secondary wood, grain runs from side to side. Rabbet three sides to fit in grooves in drawer sides and front

Examples of Good Wood Choice

A curved chair leg will look best with visible grain that follows the curve, and that is also better structurally. A curved leg with grain that goes against the curve will have "short grain" and will be much weaker. The patterns in the grain are a good clue to the structural in many cases. A frame-and-panel door will generally look best with the frame made from quartersawn lumber, with its straight lines. And this wood choice is ideal for minimizing the cross-grain stresses on the mortise-and-tenon joints.

Rift-sawn legs look great with straight grain on all four sides, and this balances the wood movement equally between the two joints. The bookmatched panels for a door are a purely visual choice – the panels are usually thinner than the stiffer frame that surrounds them to control the tendency to warp, and the construction should allow for the expansion and contraction of the panel in the frame.

This is the kind of board breaking you should try to avoid. The grain here runs across the bottom of this leg along the break line. This makes for a weak leg that is prone to break.

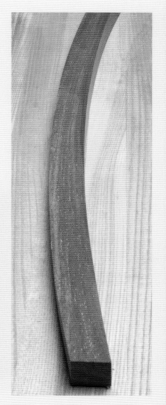

This leg is much stronger, because the grain runs with the curve.

stresses to build up in the wood. This abnormal growth is called reaction wood.

These stressed areas of the wood expand and contract with moisture variation at a very different rate than "normal," non-stressed wood. The internal stress will generally reveal itself through dramatic distortion in the wood. Try to avoid boards with major knots (remnants of large branches, which are under stress), unusually curved grain (sometimes indicative of a distorted tree trunk) and boards that have a wooly or furry surface. Unfortunately, some reaction wood isn't apparent until you try to cut the board, at which point the wood may warp suddenly to one side, or bind tightly on the blade. There isn't much you can do with a board like this short of cutting it up into very small pieces, and it's probably not worth trying. Luckily, it's not all that common. But you're still likely to encounter one once in a while, and forewarned is forearmed in dealing with this bizarre wood.

Even without unusual growing conditions there may be parts of a tree that yield wood prone to later movement or distortion. Wood sawn from parts of the tree near major branches may have compression or tension stresses as well as grain that heads in different directions. This wood can cause similar problems with warping and distortion.

Working with Wood Visually And Structurally

Up to this point, this discussion has mostly been about wood fibers. The concept of grain has been limited to discussions of end grain, and a brief mention of plain-sawn, rift-sawn and quartersawn grain patterns. The basic properties of wood are generally easier to understand using the concept of fibers. "Grain" is a term that has a huge number of different meanings, some of which are relevant to the discussion of wood behavior, and others of which are not. Certainly, one of the meanings of grain is a synonym for the fibers we've been discussing so far. But grain also describes how the pattern of growth rings appears when we cut boards out of the tree, the overall appearance of the board (also known as figure), how the fibers are oriented in the board, various wood defects and more. R. Bruce Hoadley, in his definitive book, *Understanding Wood*, lists more than 50 different usages of the word grain related to woodworking, falling into 10 different categories! These include: Long Grain, Side Grain, End Grain, Flat-sawn or Plain-sawn Grain, Quartersawn Grain, Rift-sawn Grain,

Curly Grain, Rowed Grain, and Highly Figured Grain.

Using the wood's grain to its fullest advantage is an interesting combination of visual design and engineering. Carefully chosen wood grain can enhance the overall visual effect of the piece. But it is equally important to consider the structural and behavioral characteristics of each piece of wood as it will function in the piece. Fortunately, most of the time, the appearance and the structure of the grain go hand in hand.

Color Changes

Most wood changes color as it ages. This can be a pleasant surprise, as you might find when cherry ages from the initial pale salmon color to a rich, dark reddish-brown. It can also be a great disappointment, as when purpleheart or padauk go from brilliant purple or red to a fairly ordinary brown. The color change process is a combination of photosensitivity and oxidization – exposure to light and to oxygen. Different woods change in different ways. But almost all of them change over time. Many get darker (cherry, mahogany), some get lighter (walnut), some yellow (maple, ash), others change colors (purpleheart, padauk). Most woods will eventually lose color and look bleached out if left exposed to full sun for a long time. Be aware of the potential for change as you design with wood.

Working with Wood – Joinery

Traditional woodworking techniques arose out of a deep awareness of how wood behaves. And the tradition of working with wood goes back thousands of years. Traditional joints and construction techniques take advantage of wood's strengths, and for the most part, try to minimize its weaknesses. And although there have been many advances in woodworking, the only real improvements in these techniques have been in methods for cutting wood. Many of the modern advances in technique are advances only in speed (think dowel construction), and are actually less effective joinery. There are a few cases where older techniques come up short today; moisture-related wood movement was not always quite as much of a factor hundreds of years ago – before central heating – as it is now. But we can learn from and try to avoid the few techniques that ultimately led to problems.

All traditional wood joinery relies on the basic properties of wood that we've discussed already: wood's fibrous nature and its tendency to expand and contract with changes in atmospheric moisture content. The basic principles of joining wood are:

1. Join fibers to fibers (end grain doesn't count)
2. Create as much good glue surface (fiber-to-fiber surfaces) as possible
2. Create some sort of mechanical connection if possible

Raising Dents With Moisture

Fibers that have been compressed can often be restored to their original state with moisture. This means that you can often fix a dent with a little bit of water. It's more effective if you combine water and heat, in the form of steam. With smaller dents, you can apply a drop of water to the problem, then heat the water with the tip of a clothes iron or a soldering iron. You can steam out larger dents by applying a damp cloth to the surface, and then ironing over the dented area with a clothes iron. Make sure the wood is dry before you attempt to smooth out the surface again.

Dents are all too common in the shop, but they're usually easy to remove if you rely on the tendency of wood to swell back up if you force moisture into the cells.

Put a drop of water in the dent to start the repair.

Just add heat. Here, a soldering iron heats up the moistened wood and swells up the fibers.

Examples of the Major Joints and How They Compare

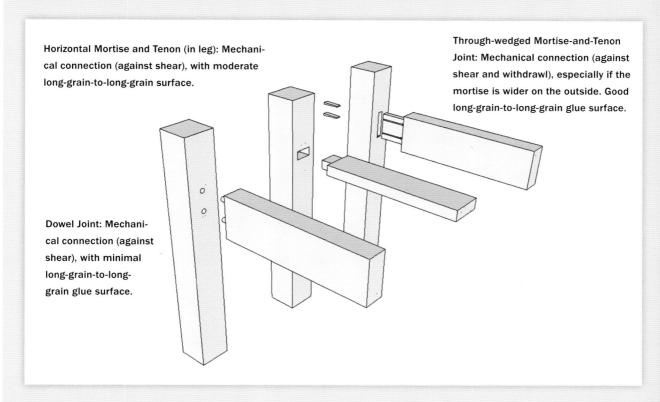

Horizontal Mortise and Tenon (in leg): Mechanical connection (against shear), with moderate long-grain-to-long-grain surface.

Through-wedged Mortise-and-Tenon Joint: Mechanical connection (against shear and withdrawl), especially if the mortise is wider on the outside. Good long-grain-to-long-grain glue surface.

Dowel Joint: Mechanical connection (against shear), with minimal long-grain-to-long-grain glue surface.

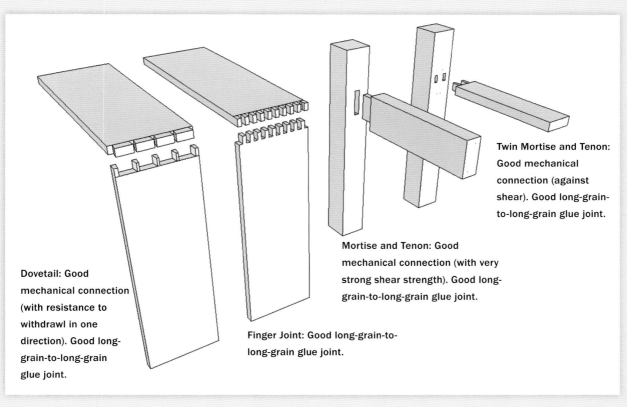

Twin Mortise and Tenon: Good mechanical connection (against shear). Good long-grain-to-long-grain glue joint.

Mortise and Tenon: Good mechanical connection (with very strong shear strength). Good long-grain-to-long-grain glue joint.

Dovetail: Good mechanical connection (with resistance to withdrawl in one direction). Good long-grain-to-long-grain glue joint.

Finger Joint: Good long-grain-to-long-grain glue joint.

Designs That Have Evolved to Deal With Wood Movement

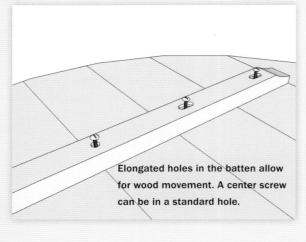

Elongated holes in the batten allow for wood movement. A center screw can be in a standard hole.

The panel has room to expand and contract in the grooves of the frame. Do not glue the panel in place; it must be free to move. It can be fixed with glue or a pin in the center, however.

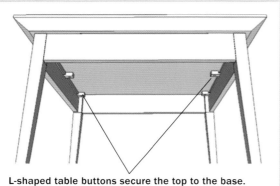

L-shaped table buttons secure the top to the base. The tongues on the table buttons fit into grooves in the aprons on both ends of the table. Screws secure the buttons to the underside of the top, but still allow the top to expand and contract.

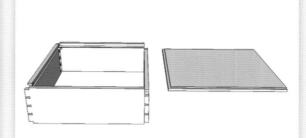

The back of the drawer is narrower than the front and sides. The drawer bottom can expand out the back if necessary.

3. Minimize the effects of wood movement

4. Avoid short grain

(See "Designs That Have Evolved...," p. 26)

It even pays to remember these principles when using fasteners such as nails and screws with wood. These provide their own mechanical fastening, but all of the other principles still apply.

Just what happens when you hammer a nail into a board depends on the shape of the nail, how that shape relates to the fiber direction in the board and even where on the board you place the nail. For the most part, the tip of the nail either slices through or wedges apart fibers, then bends them over and compresses them to make room for the nail as it pushes into the wood.

Nail two boards together with the grain at right angles, using more than a single nail, and you should certainly be aware of cross-grain wood movement issues. Nails may accommodate some wood movement by compressing nearby fibers and pulling out a little bit, but they will also loosen up over time as a result of this accommodation.

Screws are probably a little better at holding boards together, but only if you're screwing into the fibers from the side. They will also be less accommodating of wood movement, because although they may compress adjacent fibers, they won't easily pull out of a piece that is trying to move. The best approach to allow cross-grain movement when screwing boards together is to create elongated pilot holes in the board that takes the heads of the screws. (See illustrations above)

But just because screws are less likely to pull out doesn't mean that they won't loosen up over time. Screws (and nails) don't change from season to season, but the wood, of course, does. When the wood expands in wetter months, the fibers will want to swell up. Because the fasteners don't accommodate that, the wood (between threads in particular) will have to compress. When the wood shrinks back, fasteners will loosen up due to both shrinkage and compressed fibers.

Screwing down into end grain is a problem. That's because the screw threads actually cut the end grain fibers into very short sections. These short sections are then subject to the typical problems of short-grain wood; they can easily shear off. And that's exactly what they will do when the screw is either screwed down too tightly or is subject to force pulling it out. And because we normally use screws with the intention of resisting that very force, screwing into end grain is not recommended. There is a work-around solution: Drill a hole for a dowel through the face of board you would like to screw into from the end; insert the dowel and then screw from the end of the board into the dowel. (Fig. 1-14)

Either fastener is capable of splitting a board if applied close to the end of a board. Beyond the fastener is "short grain," which is more likely to split apart than to compress to make room for the nail.

Coping With Wood-movement Issues

The best way to deal with wood movement is to start thinking about it right from the start. This process often begins before you even get to the lumberyard. You should look carefully at the plans (or your design) for the project and decide what wood grain will work best for each part – visually and structurally. Make up a cutlist with notes on ideal wood choices, so when you start to pick through boards you'll have a very clear idea of exactly what you need, and where each board is going to go in your project.

What should you look for? It's always better to avoid wood with the highest potential for problems. Check the end grain for significant growth-ring curvature and the rest of the board for unruly grain. Your goal should be boards with relatively straight, even grain (unless you're

after a highly figured board for visual reasons). Check every board by sighting down the edge to see if it is straight. Sometimes you can get away with a board with some overall bow if you plan to cut the board up into short pieces. Do you want a specific grain orientation for certain parts? Make sure to mentally cut up your boards (or make a quick sketch to diagram your intentions) to see if you can get the desired pieces. As you become more experienced at this, you'll find it easier to see how to get what you want out of the wood. For example, the outer edges of wider boards can provide you with wood that is ideally suited for legs, because the end grain tends to run at about a 45° angle, and the four faces of the legs will then all have mostly straight, rift grain.

You should let your wood adjust to the basic climate it will experience when it is in place as a piece of furniture. If your shop is climate controlled, this can be as simple as stacking the wood up in your shop with thin strips of wood between the boards so that air can circulate freely around the boards (this is called stickering). (Fig. 1-15) If you work in a damp basement, outdoor shed or other space with conditions that are different than a typical home, it's better to let the wood acclimate somewhere in a controlled environment (unless the furniture is going into a damp basement). Leaving the wood for a week or two will give it some time to reach equilibrium with the surrounding air before you start to work on it, and will save headaches later.

As you begin to mill your lumber to size, you will often release some inherent stresses in the wood. Don't be surprised if there is some additional movement. Knowing that this will happen, you can plan to mill your wood a little bit oversized, let the wood sit for a couple of days to settle down, and then mill it again to final size. This "double milling" process is not something to do on every part of every project, but if there are critical parts (door frames or any other parts that you need to keep flat come to mind) you should definitely plan on it.

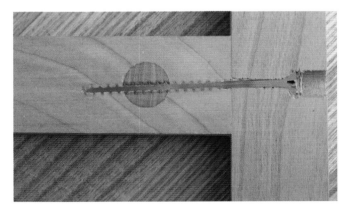

Fig. 1-14 - The dowel here in this cross-section greatly improves this screw joint by giving the screw long-grain fibers to grab.

Fig. 1-15 - Stickering a pile of wood allows air to flow evenly around all of the boards which allows for even moisture exchange.

TWO

USING YOUR BODY CORRECTLY

Have you ever thought about how you stand at your workbench? That may be more important to your ability to do accurate work than the quality of your tools. Why is that? Because first and foremost among the tools you use in woodworking is your body. Our bodies are complex "machines," composed of levers, pulleys, fulcrums and hinges, which can either enhance or detract from how you are able to work with your tools. How you use your body is actually more important than any of the "external" tools you might have.

How much attention do you pay your body's role? It isn't so much that you need bulk up your muscles or increase your endurance. But issues of balance, efficiency, alignment, proper application of force and ways to increase control are all critical to getting the most out of your body and improving the level of your craftsmanship.

Some people seem to be able to pick up a new tool, or for that matter, a new sport, and master it effortlessly. Others find these things far more difficult. Someone who pick things up more quickly tends to have a much greater awareness of his or her body and how it works. This body awareness may seem effortless in those lucky few, but it is certainly something that can be learned and improved, no matter how much or little you start with.

Woodworking "performance" is all about control. You need to maximize the control you have over your tools to do your best work. In addition, almost everything you do as you work with a piece of wood involves the application of some force to either the tool or the workpiece in order to cut, shape or smooth it into its final form. It's the controlled application of force that matters. How your body is positioned in relation to the tool or workpiece is crucial. How you use your body in that position will either increase or reduce the force you can apply and improve or hamper the control you have over your movements.

Form

An athlete looking to improve his or her performance will often work on form – on finding the most efficient, powerful and controlled way to use the body. The science of athletic performance has examined ever more successful athletes and has determined that certain ways of running, swinging a bat, golf club, or tennis racket, throwing a baseball, shooting a basketball, pedaling a bicycle, etc. lead to better results. An athlete will practice over and over, looking to be sure the ideal form becomes a natural part of how he or she performs.

Although woodworkers rarely talk about form, it is no less important. How you use your body affects everything. Using your body properly will help you increase your safety, control, power and accuracy. Using your body incorrectly makes it significantly harder to achieve any of these. Interestingly enough, this applies not just to hand-tool work, but is equally true for machine work. Good form is just as important on the table saw, the jointer and even the router, as it is with a chisel, handplane or tenon saw. And on the machines, proper form can be a matter of safety as well.

Balance

A balanced position is the starting point for most woodworking tasks. And that position should be able to keep you in balance throughout any movement you'll need to make as a part of your task. Obviously, when you're standing upright with your feet together you're not at risk for falling over. But this is a static position, and it doesn't work well for keeping your balance throughout a range of motions. So the fundamental starting position for woodworking is a slightly more versatile stance. Place your feet shoulder width apart, with one foot pointing forward, and the other behind and aiming off to the side at 45° to 60°. (Fig. 2-1) Your knees should be slightly bent and your hips forward. This is very much like the basic, neutral stance for many sports. As my son, an avid Tae Kwan Do practitioner and instructor pointed out, it is exactly the same as his "basic fighting stance." This "basic woodworking stance" is a position that allows for a wide range of motion in all directions with great balance. Almost everything that you do in the shop will benefit from this stance.

What do you do when a balanced stance just doesn't work for a specific task? Move closer to the work, if possible, so you're not reaching beyond your balance. You can also add a point of stability. This is common at the workbench, but it also works well with stationary power tools. Brace yourself against your workbench, and you can lean in for better alignment or power as you do certain types of work. (Fig. 2-2) Brace against the edge of the jointer or table saw, and you can maintain your balance as you apply the proper force to finish the cut. This may seem counterintuitive on these machines that you might otherwise be tempted to stand back from. But it actually puts you in a much safer position.

It's not always as useful, but there are some situations where can hook your foot around a leg or base of your workbench as well. This can help with your balance or the ability to push in certain directions, and therefore the control you have over your body.

You should also keep in mind that you can and should adjust the position of the workpiece to allow you to keep your body in good position. It seems obvious to point this out, but it's commonly ignored. A few seconds of moving, rotating or raising or lowering a piece can save you from contorting your body to get into a position to do your work. It may save you some lower back pain. And it may even increase your accuracy. Get in the habit of noticing your body position in relation to your work. Once you start paying attention, you'll finding that making adjustments to the workpiece is much easier on your body than contorting yourself to accommodate poorly positioned work. It's usually more efficient and accurate, too.

Never work beyond your balance point. If you are off balance in the shop it will cause serious problems with control and, more importantly, safety.

Balance in Motion

You rarely stay in one position as you work. Movement is an essential part of most of what we do. As you might expect, your movements, whether with tools or with wood, should be smooth and steady, balanced and controlled. This means more than just normal walking, just as standing at the bench to do your work involves more than simply standing there. Balanced movement, especially when you have to move while controlling a board or a tool, involves a smooth transfer of weight as you move from foot to foot and keeping your weight low (bent knees). This will help you apply consistent pressure to keep a long board against the fence at the table saw, or a handplane against a board at your bench.

Fig. 2-1 - The basic woodworking stance.

Fig. 2-2 - You get even more stability when you brace against a bench or tool.

Accounting For the Way the Body Moves

The mechanics of how the body moves is also a factor in woodworking. Joints rotate and pivot, twist or turn only in specific ways. For example, the elbow is basically a so-phisticated hinge that allows the lower arm to pivot in one plane, and also to rotate in a limited way. The shoulder allows for rotation and pivoting within its own limits. Each of your joints has a very specific impact on how you are

The Basic Woodworking Stance

The basic woodworking stance will not, by itself, change your woodworking. But it seems like most good woodworkers rely on something like this for most of their work. This is because it works. It sets up your body well for the majority of task. This is true not only for chiseling, sawing and handplaning, but also when using the table saw, jointer, band saw and other power tools.

It's not that the basic woodworking stance is always required. It's simply that using your body well most often falls back on certain things, and this is one of them. Don't feel like you immediately have to change the way you work in the shop. But start paying attention to proper use of your body, and you may find this posi-tion to be one that puts you in the best position for your work while allowing for more efficient, powerful and accurate use of your body.

able to move. You want to take into account the way these capabilities and limitations affect your movement as you work. Once you're aware of these natural tendencies of the body to work in certain ways, you can then work on modifying the movements to minimize problems or take advantage of specific body mechanics to ensure more accurate work.

If you're sanding a board with a side-to-side motion, for example, you should realize that the natural tendency of your arm when it moves from side to side is to move in an arc. (Fig. 2-3) That's how your arm moves as you pivot from either the elbow or the shoulder. Moving the sandpaper this way will leave some cross-grain scratches on the wood as part of the arc-shaped movement. You can compensate by modifying that motion and adding in elbow and wrist movement to get a straighter line (which will take some concentration and practice), or by changing the orientation of the piece (or yourself) so that you're sanding forward and back instead of from side to side. This is a more natural straight motion.

Fig. 2-3 - The natural pivoting motions of the shoulder naturally lead to a curved stroke with the sandpaper.

The back-and-forth motion doesn't solve all problems, however. When moving your hand or hands forward and back on a surface (as when sanding directly away from you), there is a tendency to change the angle of your hands; the wrist joint flexes more when your hand comes closer to your body, and straightens out as you move farther away. This isn't a factor at all when you're sanding, but if you're sharpening by hand, you're likely to change the bevel angle as you move. There are ways around this problem, too, moving forward and back more from your feet and keeping your upper body still.

You can take advantage of the natural pivoting of your arm when using a marking gauge. If you pull the marking gauge toward your body, your natural tendency will be to push it harder against the work as it comes closer. Push it away and the natural pivoting of the arm will be more likely to take the gauge away from the work.

Force, Control and Alignment

It's almost always true that you apply force and exert control separately. Most often, force is applied with the lower body, and control with the hands and arms. Obviously, nothing is completely independent when you're doing this; the force has to go through your core (abdomen), upper body, arms and hands to get to your fingers. Concentrating on force and control as separate jobs for different parts of the body will help your body make the appropriate adjustments.

One of the most important factors connecting force and control is proper alignment. Alignment helps to avoid wasting force; it's more efficient to have your body in proper alignment with the work. Think about trying to move a heavy object; you want to be directly behind the object and pushing in the direction you want it to go, not off to one side and pushing at an angle. When your body is not aligned properly, there is additional work that needs to be done by your muscles as they make the corrections that need to be made in the angles of the joints.

Alignment is also essential for accuracy. Your joints are a series of linkages that provide you with remarkable flexibility in how you move. But these linkages can also introduce lots of hard-to-control motion. It's certainly possible to learn how to work this way, and there are situations where you will have to make do (cramped quarters inside a case, an awkward angle for planing, etc.) But reducing the number of joint movements that need to be controlled makes it far easier to achieve accuracy. And reducing the amount of inefficient (and therefore harder) work can also improve accuracy. The harder you work in any situation, the less likely you are to be accurate.

Misalignment introduces inaccurate movements. If you're trying to make an accurate cut with a handsaw, you need to move the saw back and forth in a very straight line. If your forearm is not lined up with the back of the saw, your shoulder and wrist will have to continuously change angles to compensate (wasting energy as well). (Fig. 2-4) While it may be possible to do that, it's much easier to keep the joints aligned so that you only really have to move the shoulder and bend the elbow a little in a single plane. (Fig. 2-5) That motion will naturally be linear. And there's the

Fig. 2-4 - My forearm isn't lined up with the saw, which means both my wrist and shoulder have to rotate when I cut.

Fig. 2-5 - Here, the saw and my forearm line up correctly. I'm a little further off to the side in order to accomplish this.

added benefit of transmitting the force straight through the wrist, which no longer has to flex out of alignment and can stay straight.

Movement through aligned joints is important in more than just handsawing. It's a key component in working at the jointer and table saw, and when using a chisel, handplane and many other tools.

Generating Force

We've determined that proper alignment of your limbs is important if you are to apply force efficiently. But where

does that force come from? It depends on what you're trying to do. But most of the time, more of the body should be involved than you might think. The general principle is to rely on your larger muscles or muscle groups to apply the force.

Because it has your body's strongest muscles, your lower body should be working a lot of the time. This is another reason why you need a balanced position and controlled movement. Whether it's handplaning or pushing a board over the jointer, the lower body actually should be doing the bulk of the work. And even sharpening by hand

Basic Principles for Applying Force

- **Use your weight and proper position, not strength.**
- **Use bigger muscles rather than smaller ones.**
- **Don't be lazy about changing your position or that of the workpiece so you can take advantage of either of the first two rules.**
- **Use mechanical advantage wherever you can find it.**
- **Don't over-reach.**
- **Don't work harder than you have to (this will impact accuracy). Any time you have to push or strain, try to remove too much material at once or you get tense about something you're doing, it will impact your accuracy; it's extremely difficult to work hard and precisely at the same time.**

Fig. 2-6 - Cutting too hard (or fast) with a machine makes a mess of the cut. I cut the block in front too quickly on the table saw. I fed the back piece through the saw at the proper speed.

works better if you're using your lower body for the overall movement. To take advantage of this, you need that balanced stance.

Of course, it's not always the lower body. Paring with a chisel is usually upper-body work, but it's not solely hand or arm work. Working from the shoulders, or even bending at the waist to transfer upper body weight, is far more effective.

Stop Working So Hard

Working hard and working accurately do not go together. This isn't a call to improve your accuracy by lazing around in the shop. But you need to ease up when accuracy matters. This is easy to see when using a chisel – if you try to take off too much wood with each cut, you're much more likely to have the cut go astray as you struggle to

get through the wood. You'll also be liable to compress or split the wood, sometimes disastrously. Paring or chopping smaller amounts of wood will be more controlled and more accurate. You can certainly whale away when you're just wasting away material and the work doesn't have to be precise. Just ease up when the work gets critical.

Interestingly enough, working hard and accuracy don't go together on machines either. Straining to support your workpiece will mean you have less ability to control it. But more importantly, when you push a machine or cutter to work too hard (cutting too fast or too deep, for example) it will have an impact on cut quality and accuracy as well. (Fig. 2-6 & 2-7) You have to pay attention to tell when a machine is working too hard, but once you're aware of the problem, you'll quickly learn what works and what doesn't.

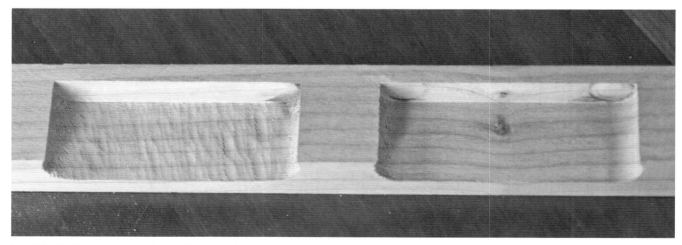

Fig. 2-7 - Cutting too aggressively with the router caused problems both visible (note the rough surface) and invisible (it is measurably wider) in the mortise on the left (sliced in half lengthwise). The otherwise-identical mortise at the right was routed at an appropriate speed.

Increasing Your Control

If the larger muscles and muscle groups provide the bulk of the force needed to do most tasks, your fingers, hands and lower arms provide the control. In most situations, your fingers and hands shouldn't be asked to do both.

Control can mean many different things. There's the control over tool location, which is important for chisel placement. There's control over the angle at which you hold a tool, which can be critical during sharpening or chisel work. There's control over pressure distribution, an important part of successful handplane use. There's no secret formula for all of this control. But there are common denominators. Control requires concentration. And not surprisingly, control also requires proper hand and body position.

Control over placement comes the closest to having a simple answer. All of us have been training our hands for detailed work since very early childhood. Writing requires an extraordinary amount of precise control, and it's a good idea to tap into that skill. Use one hand (it doesn't have to be your writing hand) to provide that high-level control. This means holding the tool more or less like you would hold a pencil, close to the business end. Your other hand (often in conjunction with your upper body) can provide the necessary force. Keep your detail hand grounded on the work if possible. You don't write with your hand up off the paper, and there's no reason to try to control a chisel or other similar tool that way, either. (Fig. 2-8) To keep good control of an angle you have to maintain your position well. And this involves more than just your hands. You'll usually have to "lock up" your upper body, holding the elbow and forearm of one or both arms against your body.

Control over pressure distribution, so important to handplane use, is the least obvious, largely because it's not something you can see. It's a feel, an awareness that you'll need to work to build. Fortunately, there are some simple exercises that can help. Body position is still critical.

Try planing a short board (³⁄₄" thick, 4" or 5" wide, and about 8" long) against a single bench dog. (Fig. 2-9) You'll discover right away that you need to push down more on the front of the plane as you get started, and on the back of the plane as you get to the end of the board. You also need to maintain good side-to-side balance. Keep at it until you don't tip the board over at the end of the cut.

Another exercise in good control over hand pressure is planing a convex board with a smoothing plane. (Fig. 2-10) This gets harder as the plane gets bigger. Keeping the plane cutting means you have to constantly adjust the balance between your hands. Try to get long, continuous shavings.

Where control most often falls apart is when you start to apply force. This is where the rest of your body is so important. If you want to hold your upper body position carefully to maintain accuracy, you have to rely on body weight

Fig. 2-8 - The pencil grip for a chisel.

Fig. 2-9 - Planing a short board upright against a single bench dog is a good way to learn about balance and pressure when planing.

Fig. 2-10 - To keep the cutting edge on the wood when you plane a convex curve with a straight plane, you have to learn to balance the pressure between your hands.

or your lower body to apply force. It's also very important to limit your cut to what can be done without messing up your control.

Despite the fact that force and control are often handled by separate parts of the body, they still happen at the same time, and are interdependent. Luckily, you're pretty well wired to combine different types of motion easily (the old walking and talking thing). And if it's not easy right off the bat, it's something that you'll get used to fairly quickly. If you find it too much to think about at once, work on getting the movement responsible for force in place first, and go over it a few times. Once you don't have to think about it as much, you can concentrate on what you really need to pay attention to: the control stuff.

There are some tasks that seem to require concentration on both force and control at once. Feeding awkward boards through the table saw and over the jointer come immediately to mind. Both of these call for steady feed rates despite shifting hand positions and less-than-optimal alignment for applying force. These situations simply require practice (try a couple of test runs with the machine off) so you can get used to the awkward set-up.

Containment/ Proximity

Control, accuracy and force all diminish when you work farther from your torso. And the farther you go, the more that's true. So most of your work should be contained within a relatively small area around your body where your strength and control are at their peak. The sweet spot is not right up next to your torso, but it's pretty close. You should find that your elbows don't get all that far from your body, except as you finish up certain longer movements. You may have to play around a little to see just what works best for you.

Look closely at the photos of hand planing on p.64-67, and notice that despite the large motion of planing, the elbow of my pushing hand never strays far from my body.

There are exceptions to this, but far fewer than you might imagine.

Working in the Right Position, Working at the Right Height

It's extremely important that you position your workpiece so you can do whatever needs to be done on it comfortably and effectively. Important as this advice might be, it is easily overlooked or ignored. This of the one of the main

Fig. 2-11 - The Noden Adjust-A-Bench gives you the flexibility to work at the right height for almost any task.

reasons you need an appropriate workbench or work station; you need flexibility in positioning and holding a variety of pieces for all types of work. It's equally important, and even more easily overlooked, that you consider the height at which you work as well.

Different tasks in the shop are best done at different heights. For example, planing usually works best at a height that is in the range between your knuckle and your wrist height as you stand with your arms comfortably at your side. This allows you to use both your body weight and lower body strength effectively as you plane. But a height that works well for planing may seem too low for joinery work, which can be much more comfortable and

accurate at stomach-to-chest height. That height allows you to position your body well for tasks such as sawing, measuring, marking, chiseling and routing without constantly leaning over and stressing your back. Certain kinds of detail work are better even higher than that, at chest height. Working at the right height will certainly save your back and neck. You'll also see better and you'll be able to apply the proper amount of force or control for the specific task as well.

How can you quickly and easily accommodate the tasks you'll do at these heights in your shop?

The easiest solution is simple denial. Just go ahead and do the work. The human body is very adaptable, and you'll

Fig. 2-12 - A shop-made benchtop bench (a small workbench that you clamp on top of your existing bench) provides workholding and a surface at an ideal height for detail work.

do just fine; at least for a while. But you'll probably start to feel the effects of working at a less-than-optimal height – and you'll feel it quicker and you'll feel it more as you get older.

You can pull up a stool that's an appropriate height to position yourself at a better height in relation to your work at your bench. But sitting may impact your ability to do work that would otherwise benefit from good body alignment or application of force from stronger muscles.

Most workbenches are designed as something of a compromise, because there's so much variation in size from person to person, and plenty of variation in ideal heights for various tasks. There is no real all-purpose bench out

there. There is an adjustable-height workbench that can be raised or lowered as needed; the Noden Adjust-A-Bench is available as a complete workbench or as just a base mechanism. (Fig. 2-11) The Noden bench is rigid and relatively easy to raise and lower on a ratcheting mechanism. Some people have enough shop space for more than one workbench. In that case, separate planing (relatively low) and joinery (relatively high) benches are a good idea. Perhaps the best solution is to make (or purchase) a benchtop solution: either a miniature workbench or an auxiliary vise that can be clamped to the top of your main workbench to hold a workpiece at a higher height. (Fig. 2-12 & 2-13)

Whatever solution you choose, it should be something

that you can turn to quickly and easily. You don't need to do this for every little task that comes up (denial definitely works), but it's good to avoid the things that are going to hurt your back or neck if you're at them for a while. And you'll see better and have more control as well.

Staying Relaxed

It's common to tense up when trying to learn a new way of doing something that involves physical movement. Adding in the thought that you should relax is not always beneficial (although sometimes it helps). Instead, try to break down the task into smaller components and work on these until you can do them without tension. Then add in the next component. It's particularly helpful to commit to working on the muscle memory separate from the accuracy and detail. (See chapter 11 on practicing for a more complete discussion.) Don't stress about accuracy right away, either. It comes from a few things: using your body correctly and without added movement or tension; an awareness of exactly where you need to cut (see chapter 7); experi-

menting to see how you can best put these things together and then practice. Sometimes lots of practice. Most people don't expect to be able to go out on a golf course and play a respectable round without having practiced for years. Don't place that kind of burden on yourself and expect perfect dovetails right away either. It won't take nearly as long as learning to play golf. But it does take good form, a solid concept of what you need to do and plenty of practice.

Once you start to see how you should use your body and understand what it is that you're trying to do on a specific task, you'll be on the path to discovering the best way for you to do it. You should always experiment with how you do things. Partly, this is out of necessity – every piece of wood, every task and every project is a little bit different. But knowing just what it is you're supposed to do, and paying attention to how your body is accomplishing (or not accomplishing) what you want to do, you should be able to make quick adjustments that will keep you on the right path.

Fig. 2-13 - Benchcrafted's Moxon vise holds boards for dovetailing (and other work) at a perfect height.

THREE

LEARNING TO SEE BETTER

There's a vast difference between the information that your eyes collect and what you process and understand of that information. Why is this?

In order to make sense of the visual world, we learn from infancy to take a small amount of the visual information that our eyes collect and identify it. We learn that certain patterns and shapes indicate a chair, a table, a dog, a cat or a particular individual's face. And we learn to make these interpretations with the minimal amount of visual data. In other words, we learn to take shortcuts. We don't need to pay attention to every freckle or pore on a person's face in order to identify them, and it's likely we don't even notice those things. This has great advantages. There's no need to waste brain "processing power" examining all of the details of an object in order to know what something is, or how it may affect us.

But this also means we tend to ignore a great deal of the available information. As craftsmen, much of this information is meaningful, however. So we need to learn to observe more of it. In some cases, we also need to learn to actually see more of it.

In truth, seeing and observing are different, and both are important to your woodworking. Learning to see better is mostly a question of technical issues – things such as improved lighting, better viewing angles and perhaps some corrective lenses if necessary. It's also a question of what you actually look at. Observing more involves not only knowing what to actively look for, but also knowing how to interpret what you observe. And this means increasing your awareness and your knowledge of a variety of issues.

Because this is a learned skill, the more you do it, the better you'll get at it. That's good news, because learning to see and observe more are crucial to better woodworking.

Lighting

Good lighting in the shop is important for doing good work. And it will get more and more important as you get older. Like it or not, your eyesight will deteriorate with age, and you'll need more and more light to help you see adequately as you work. Strangely, the vision changes that you experience as you get older don't seem to hide the problems in the finished pieces; they just make it harder to see them while you're working.

Adequate lighting may become more and more important as you age – but flexibility in the way you illuminate your work will always be a major help. In addition to the typical battery of fluorescent lamps hanging from the ceiling, I've become a big fan of adjustable task lighting. These are articulated-arm desk lamps that I can move around and adjust easily. I've also mounted them in a variety of flexible ways. Most of my benches have ½" holes into which I can drop the post at the base of the lamp. I've also made up some bench dogs with ½" holes so I can mount a lamp in a bench dog, and therefore into any of the bench dog holes. (Fig. 3-1) And for other locations, I've got a wooden handscrew with a ½" mounting hole as well. This can be clamped to other benches, cabinets or tools as needed. All of this allows me to position a light so it can bring out the most detail under almost any cir-

Fig. 3-1 - Dropping the post of a swing-arm lamp into a ½" hole in a bench dog allows me to move the light wherever I need it on my bench.

Fig. 3-2 - A hole in a set of handscrews means I can attach the lamp anywhere I can secure the clamp.

Guidelines for Proper Lighting in a Shop

Although most people cobble together a "just good enough" array of lights for their shops, it's a not a bad idea to put a little more thought (and money) into your basic lighting scheme. A good target would be something in the neighborhood of 50 to 75 foot-candles (a foot-candle is a standard measure of light intensity). This is probably quite a bit brighter than the average shop. There are plenty of free lighting calculators available online that can help you figure out how many light fixtures you'll need to produce that level of light in your shop.

cumstance. (Fig. 3-2)

Why is this flexibility so important? Low, raking light reveals and accentuates details that might be completely invisible under more diffuse overhead light. Faint scribed lines, irregular edges and surface problems all show up dramatically. (Fig. 3-3 & 3-4) Many of these problems will become quite visible once finish goes on the wood; reflective surfaces show even the smallest problems easily. It's very important that you examine your work in the most revealing light possible.

Adjustable sources of light also give you control over shadows. You can easily move the light source if your layout lines are hiding in the shadow of a tool or another part of the workpiece.

Fig. 3-3 - A low, raking light shows up all of the surface nastiness on this board.

Fig. 3-4 - Diffuse, overhead light reveals much less.

Fig. 3-5 - Looking at a curve on end shows up lumps, bumps, and awkward parts of the curve that you'd have a much harder time seeing from the side.

There also seems to be an intangible boost in accuracy and focus when you have the lamp right up close to the work.

Viewing Angle

One of the easiest ways to see more is to change your point of view. How you choose to look at something will often control how much you see. One way to do this is to simply be sure you're looking at your work from every side. This will point out relationships and proportions that you might not otherwise be aware of. It may also point out places that you've failed to smooth, finish or refine. These things might not matter if the piece won't ever be seen from other points of view. But if your piece will be visible from all sides, you should certainly be walking all around it and inspecting it from all sides as you work. Don't just let it sit where it's located on your workbench and leave it at that.

A less obvious way to see more is to choose a low viewing angle. From a low angle, you'll have a dramatically better view of sanding scratches and other surface imperfections. You'll also get a much better sense of whether or not a board is straight, and how well and fairly curves flow. For the best possible view of these details, combine a low

viewing angle with a low raking light. Nothing will be able to hide from you. (Fig. 3-5)

The Dominant Eye

The advantages of stereo vision are fairly obvious. Depth perception is the result of processing the slight differences in visual information from our two eyes. There's also a redundancy of information that can help if there are any problems with the vision in one eye. Almost everything we do benefits from our ability to stitch together a coherent and rich picture of our surroundings out of the information from two eyes. But for certain tasks in woodworking, the information from both eyes causes some conflict. That's because your two eyes see things from different perspectives. Your brain sorts out the differences relying on the information from one eye – your dominant eye – to provide the essential part of the image you see, and filling in details of depth and a broader field of vision with the information from the other eye. When you need to align a tool precisely with a line, you need some of the information from both eyes available to you. But it's more important that you concentrate on the information from the dominant eye. This is an odd state of concentration –

Fig. 3-6 - You need to align your eye perpendicular to the layout line to get an accurate measurement.

Determining Your Dominant Eye

Which of your eyes is the dominant eye? Point at a distant object with both eyes open. Still pointing at the object, close each of your eyes in turn. With your dominant eye open, you'll still be pointing at the object. When only the other eye is open, you'll be pointing at something else.

it's not quite letting your eyes go out of focus, but it can feel a little bit like that. It's willing yourself to see more with one eye without closing the other eye. This is not an easy concept.

Parallax

Parallax is defined as the displacement of an object based on the line of sight. In other words, it is a shift in what you see based on the angle of view. This can cause numerous errors of measurement or alignment in your work. The most common problem shows up when you try to read or mark from a ruler and your eye isn't directly over and perpendicular to the markings. It's pretty easy to be off by a 64th or even a 32nd. (Fig. 3-6 & 3-7) The simplest solution is proper alignment; just make sure your dominant eye is directly over the measurement line you need. But this isn't always possible. You might try tipping the ruler up on edge, so the lines actually touch the work surface, or switching to a thinner ruler, which will reduce the possible error.

Visual Aids

Magnifying glasses, illuminated magnifiers and head-mounted magnifiers can all help you to enlarge details and see more precisely. But they all require some adjustment in hand-eye coordination as well. And although they make it easier to see in greater detail, you still have to know where to cut, and be able to make those cuts in that location. Visual aids can be an enormous help if you're having trouble seeing the details, but they are not an immediate fix for inaccurate work.

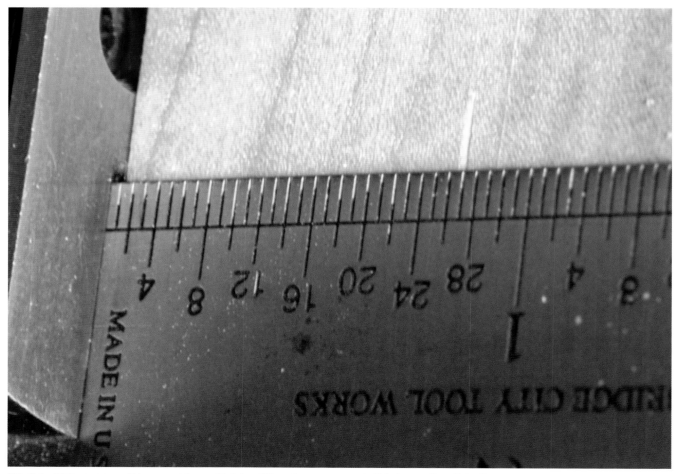

Fig. 3-7 - With your eye off to one side, you'll get a different measurement. This is parallax distortion.

"... you see, but you do not observe,"

- Sherlock Holmes to Dr. Watson
in Arthur Conan Doyle's A Scandal in Bohemia.

Where to Look

If you don't know where to look, you probably won't see what you need to see. You need to know what to watch when you work, and learn to stay focused on that. Which visual information is the most important? This is partly based on experience, but it's also based on common sense. Don't just look at something because it captures your attention. Look at it because it's a matter of safety or accuracy. There are plenty of situations where there are many different things to keep track of. But you should still be able to prioritize, and devote more attention to the issues of safety and accuracy. For example, when ripping wood on the table saw, it really doesn't do any good to watch the blade cut the wood. It may be darkly fascinating, but you actually don't get any important information from it. It's far more important to watch to be sure the edge of the board is tight against the rip fence, while making sure that your hands are well clear of the guards and the saw blade. These are important to both cut quality and safety.

Cutting with a handsaw, the interface between the cut and the line is your focus. More specifically, you want to watch the corner of the blade that's closest to the line as it interacts with the line, while keeping an eye on the cut as a whole, which will help you to stay on track.

Knowing what to look at is important. Maintaining your focus on these crucial things is even more important. It's not easy. It takes great concentration. But the longer you can maintain this focus the more accurately you will cut.

Observation

What do you observe when you look at a piece of wood? Do you notice how it was milled? Can you tell if it was handplaned, run through a thickness planer, sawn on a table saw or sanded? Can you tell how sharp the blade was? Or how skilled the hand planing or sanding was? Was the table saw out of alignment? Do you know what the grain is doing? Would you even think to look for any of these things?

There are many things that may be invisible to the beginning or immediate woodworker, but they all wind up being factors in the overall quality of the piece. And once the finish goes on, it's as if you've amplified all of these details. What may be invisible in raw wood may be glaringly obvious in a finished piece. All of the strategies for seeing better will help you spot problems in your work, but the most important factor is actively looking for them, and knowing what you're looking for.

What do you observe when you look at a piece of furniture? What are you looking for? It's likely you'll see the quality of the finish and the workmanship, but can you tell if some of the joints were cut by hand or by machine (look for layout lines below the aprons on hand-cut mortise and tenon joints, and scribed base lines and the proportions on dovetails)? Do you pick up on proportions and relationships of scale? Do you notice negative space? Are the curves fair? What about the overall balance of the piece?

These are all questions of substantially more than just what you see. Most of these questions presume some knowledge of design, woodworking techniques, tools and the wood itself. They involve seeking out visual information, and then taking the visual information that you've seen and putting it into context.

You build up this context from prior observations. If you don't know what a table-sawn edge looks like compared to a jointed, planed or a sanded one, you won't know how to interpret what you see. This is just as true when it comes to issues of proportion, form and design. You can work to build up your observational and interpretational skills simply by looking more closely at what you and others are doing. Every piece you look at can be an opportunity to observe and learn more.

The more you do this, the more you'll both see (because you're looking for it) and observe (because you understand what you see).

This increased awareness is a great thing. It's one of the most important steps you can take to get better. It's the most fundamental part of improvement. If you don't notice something, there's nothing at all you can do to improve it. It's worth mentioning that this is also a never-ending process. The better you get, the more you'll pay attention to, and the more you'll see. That's exciting. And it's a little bit daunting.

One way to really kick-start your awareness is to spend some time looking at furniture with someone who is better than you. It doesn't even have to be your furniture; you may be more receptive to comments if your ego isn't tied up in the critique.

None of this is to slight your other senses. As we'll see in the chapter on feedback, all of your senses play a role in better work. But humans are predominantly visual, and how and what we see is deserving of extra attention.

CHAPTER FOUR

UNDERSTANDING YOUR TOOLS

The best way to think of your tools is as extensions of your body. They give you all kinds of extraordinary power and vastly expand your ability to create. But none of that happens automatically. It's only true if you understand how the tools function and how you are supposed to work with them. What's more, we're working with wood, so you need to understand just how the tools interact with that wood. This need is more immediately obvious when working with hand tools, but it's no less true just because you add power.

If your tools are to actually become extensions of your capabilities, you'll need to make them your own. A new tool – even a very good one – just out of the box is simply the raw material for what you need. It may need to be sharpened, tweaked, and then set up, as you might do with a hand plane. Or it might need

to be leveled, aligned and then accessorized with a cross-cut sled, tenoning jig, or dado blade, as you might need to do with a table saw before it can do the various jobs you need it to do. Either way, a new tool just out of the box is not all that dissimilar from a new computer just out of the box; the computer may be exciting and new, but it won't do what you need it to do until software is installed and the data is imported.

The following discussions cover the essentials of some of the most basic tools you might want at your disposal. They include how the tools work, what's necessary for them to work well, safety and proper use. Entire books have been written about each of these tools; books filled with important information that goes well beyond the essentials covered here. All of these will increase your understanding as they build upon these essentials.

Chisels

The chisel is one of the simplest of all tools; it's essentially just a sharp wedge at the end of a handle. As is often the case, though, the simpler the tool, the greater the range of potential uses. Chisels are useful for delicate paring, for chopping, for shaping and carving, for scraping surfaces and even for prying up carpet tacks (ouch). The chisel's simplicity may lead you to believe that its use is also simple. But simple tools often require more skilled input to make them work well.

How Chisels Work

Chisels cut wood in different ways depending on the orientation of the cut relative to the fibers in a piece of wood. There are three basic grain orientations: across the ends of the fibers – end grain; crosswise to the length of the fibers – cross-grain; and in roughly the same direction as the fibers. This latter splits into two, however, and includes both with the grain, and against the grain, which cut very differently.

In any of these orientations the chisel will act like what it is, a wedge, and will either cut or separate wood fibers. Wood will be removed only if there is some place for it to go. If there is no place for the cut or separated fibers to go, the chisel will also compress them. This will happen equally to either side of the chisel.

When chiseling across end grain, the chisel is oriented perpendicular to the wood fibers. This cut is directly through the straw-like fibers. (Fig. 4-1) The main issue is compression. The fibers tend to give a little bit before they can be sliced. If the chisel isn't sharp enough, or you're trying to take tool much wood off at one time, fibers are likely to separate from one another (sometimes quite dramatically) before the chisel can cut, leaving a ragged surface. (Fig. 4-2) In addition, if you pare or chop all the way across the end of a board, you'll blow out the unsupported fibers at the far end.

Fig. 4-1 - While paring a thin shaving off the end grain, a sharp chisel slices through the ends of the fibers cleanly.

Cutting across the grain, with its edge parallel to the wood fibers, the chisel separates the fibers more than it cuts them. This is because the bond between fibers is not as strong as the fibers themselves. Close to the surface of the board, the chisel will peel off the fibers. Because the fibers are stronger than their bonds, though, you need to be aware that the fibers may peel off beyond where the chisel is cutting. (Fig. 4-3) This also means that the resulting surface may have some fibers pulled out below where you're cutting because the fibers may not be perfectly aligned with your cut. If you strike or push a chisel aligned this way aggressively into the wood, it may split the wood apart well beyond the chisel. With enough force it may even split the entire board.

Cutting with or against the grain, the chisel is perpendicular to the fibers, but moves along the fibers. This is where grain direction plays such a big role. If the cut is in the direction of the emerging fibers, the chisel will slice through the fibers cleanly. If the fibers angle up toward the chisel and against the direction of the cut, the chisel is going to wedge apart and break the fibers more easily than it will cut them. This will result in splitting below the surface, or tearing out of the fibers. (Figs. 4-4 & 4-5)

In all of these cases, the chisel needs to be sharp. The cutting angle can be different for chisels designed for different tasks. The more acute the angle, the more easily the chisel will cut. But more steeply angled edges are more fragile. A chisel used strictly for paring tends to work best at roughly a 25° angle. A mortise chisel – designed solely for chopping – is better off at closer to 35° (usually as a 5° micro-bevel on a 30° primary bevel). And chisels designed for all-purpose use do well at 30° (often a 5° micro-bevel on a 25° primary bevel).

For most furniture work, the chisel also needs a flat back (see the chapter on sharpening). Carving chisels are designed to function differently, and typically have a back bevel or a slight round over on the back edge. But for fur-

Fig. 4-2 - Getting too aggressive, even with a sharp chisel, will cause both compression failure and the tearing out of fibers.

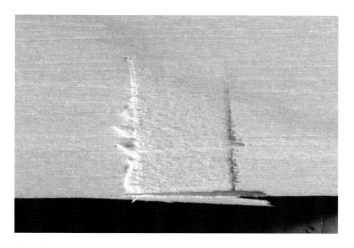

Fig. 4-3 - Paring across the grain can tear out the fibers to either side of the intended cut. It will also split off unsupported fibers at the end of the cut.

Fig. 4-4 - The chisel can easily wedge apart fibers that angle up to the surface against the direction of cut.

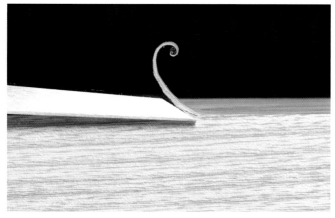

Fig. 4-5 - Fibers that are backed up by those underneath them are easier to cut cleanly.

A Good Craftsman Never Blames the Tools

As important as your tools are, it's important that you use them, and not just spend all of your time making sure that they are perfectly in order. Fussing with your tools is a terrific way to procrastinate and avoid getting any real work done. Yes, it's said that a good craftsman never blames his tools. But that doesn't mean that your tools should be blameless; it means that your skill is more important. Concentrate more on refining your skills than on refining your tools. Blameless tools are far less likely to get the job done without skill than skilled work with flawed tools.

You want to be sure that the tool(s) you need are adequate for the job at hand. But don't hide from your work by trying to get everything in the shop in order before you begin. It will never happen.

I understand the trap that's at the root of this. You know your skills aren't up to snuff, but you want to be certain that the tools aren't holding you back. Don't get pulled too deeply into this. Plan to spend at least some of the time you want to spend on the tools on your skills instead.

---

niture work, you need to know where the chisel is going as you pare or chop. And a flat back is essential for that.

Chisel Safety

Chisel safety can generally be summed up in one simple rule: keep two hands behind the edge. What does this mean? It's simple. Don't aim the chisel at yourself.

It's surprisingly tempting to hold a piece of wood in one hand and work with a chisel in your other hand. Be vigilant about this. It feels perfectly natural to do it, is surprisingly common (and often defended when pointed out), and is a very dangerous habit. See how long it takes before you discover yourself doing this. And then stop. It's a very easy and quick way to arrange for a trip to the local emergency room.

Any time you're working with a razor-sharp and completely exposed edge, you have to be careful. Always watch your hands, and be thoughtful and deliberate about chisel placement on the bench. A falling chisel can do a great deal of damage to your feet.

Chisel Techniques

How you use a chisel varies with the technique and the specific task. And with such a wide variety of techniques and tasks, there are a lot of possibilities. It comes down to much more than just how you hold the tool. To use a chisel well, your whole body needs to be positioned well.

When holding the chisel for vertical paring, hold the chisel by the handle in a kind of stabbing grip. Keep this arm tight to your body. Your other hand should be used for precise positioning. (Fig. 4-6) A grip similar to a pencil grip, with the heel of the hand resting on the workpiece is best for this. You want to be able to move the chisel in very small increments (a 64th of an inch or even less, at times). There's phenomenally good control with this type of grip, but you may find something slightly different that

works for you. Whatever you settle on, keeping your hand grounded on the work is important. You don't try to move a pencil precisely while holding on to the eraser end; don't do the equivalent when you need precise control over the chisel.

Your body should be both close to the work and well balanced, typically in the basic woodworking stance. It often helps to brace against the workbench with your

Fig. 4-6 - A good position for paring.

Fig. 4-7 - I'm in a good position to see what I'm doing, and to control and apply force to the chisel.

Fig. 4-8 - Working at the bench, I may have to lean in over it to align both my body and my eye over the chisel.

front leg, while keeping the other leg back. The chisel usually winds up beneath your neck or chin – a position that gives you good control, downward force and the ability to sight down the side of the chisel to see whether you're in position and square to the work. Your hands and arms are responsible for maintaining control, and shouldn't do much moving. The force comes primarily from your abdominal muscles, along with your shoulder and upper arm. This allows you to use your weight more than just arm strength. (Fig. 4-7)

If you're paring, you shouldn't have to force the tool. If you're struggling to make the cut it usually means you're trying to cut too much wood. And when that happens, your accuracy will typically go out the window. The chisel may wobble in your hand or you'll lose your position. You may also cause compression failure if you're paring across the

grain. Adjust your cuts accordingly.

The grip for chopping with a chisel depends on the accuracy you need. More accurate positioning calls for a pencil-like grip like you might use for paring. Holding the handle (with your hand out of harm's way from the mallet) may make it more comfortable when hitting the chisel harder for more aggressive, less critical chopping. Your body shouldn't be in quite as close to the work as when paring; you need room to swing the mallet. But you still need to position yourself or the work so you can see what needs to be seen. (Fig. 4-8)

Another common grip is to hold the chisel with the top of the handle against the heel of your hand, extending your forefinger towards the bevel. This puts the chisel in line with your forearm, and allows you to push well. (Fig. 4-9) This works well for paring horizontally. Again, the other

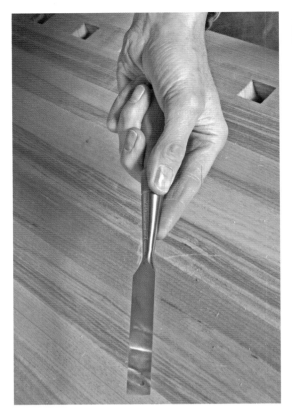

Fig. 4-9 - For paring, a good grip lines up the chisel with your forearm and allows you to push easily through the heel of your hand.

Fig. 4-10 - Paring horizontally uses a grip different from the "pencil" grip on the control hand.

hand will be for control and positioning. But the "control hand" grip is usually different from the pencil-like grip in vertical paring. Instead, try holding the chisel with your palm facing up and with your thumb on the bevel side and forefinger on the flat side of the chisel. It still helps to ground your hand; in this case, keeping the knuckles against the work will give you greater control over your movements. (Fig. 4-10)

You can use the same handle grip and a similar control-hand position for a slicing cut. This might be used to trim a projection flush with a surface. Place the chisel flat side down on the workpiece. With your thumb either on top of or next to the chisel, pivot the handle with your other hand as you push forward on the handle. Your thumb will act as the fulcrum of a lever for the side-to-side slicing movement. (Fig. 4-11)

There are times when you'll need added control over your paring. Use your "control hand" to regulate the cut, putting pressure on top of the chisel. This pressure will help keep the chisel from cutting farther than you might like. This is a great technique if you're trying to pare out

Fig. 4-11 - Slicing with the chisel is very effective for flushing a projection.

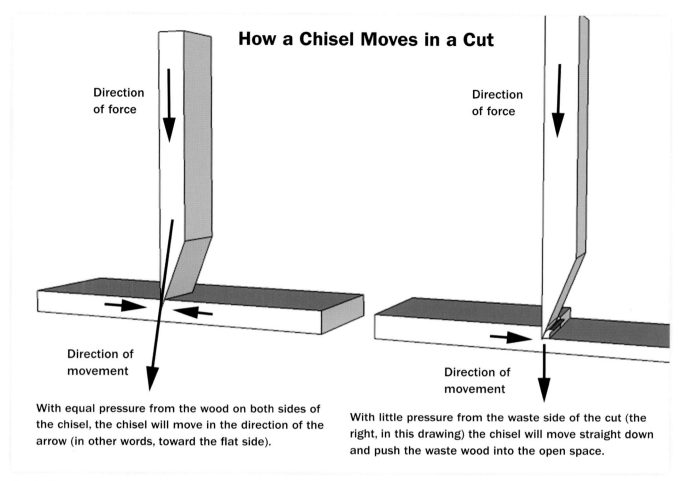

How a Chisel Moves in a Cut

Direction of force

Direction of movement

With equal pressure from the wood on both sides of the chisel, the chisel will move in the direction of the arrow (in other words, toward the flat side).

Direction of force

Direction of movement

With little pressure from the waste side of the cut (the right, in this drawing) the chisel will move straight down and push the waste wood into the open space.

Fig. 4-12

some wood next to a scribed line, but have concerns about paring too far. (Refer to Fig. 4-10)

Accurate Cuts

What determines where will the chisel go? If you take a chisel and place it on a line on a piece of wood, then tap down with a mallet, the chisel will move back over the line as it penetrates the wood. This is simple physics. The chisel moves in the direction that is exactly half of the bevel angle when there is equal resistance from both sides of the tool. (Fig. 4-12)

Moving back over the line is not typically what you're trying to do, however. In most cases, you want to chop or pare straight down. In order for that to happen, the back of the chisel must be flat (if there's any bevel or curve to the chisel back, there is no way of knowing just where the chisel will go), and you have to meet one of two additional conditions. First is that you pare or chop next to an open space, so that the wood on the bevel side is free to be pushed out of the way and won't push back against the bevel (in other words, there can only a little bit of wood to chop or pare out of the way, and that little bit has to have a

place it can go). Or you need to do something to physically prevent the chisel from "backing up." That something can be the edge of a rabbet, a block clamped tightly in place (it helps to glue a piece of sandpaper to the underside of the block to increase the friction), or some other immovable object that will overcome the force of the wood pushing against the bevel of the chisel as it penetrates the wood. This points to a common rule of chisel use: the bevel generally faces the waste side of the cut.

Cutting straight down is good, but straight down exactly on a line is even better. Chisels do this especially well when paired with marking gauges or marking knives. The scribed lines made by either layout tool actually give you with the beginnings of a perfect line. You can start either by removing most of the wood on the waste side, then chisel straight down on the line as described above, or you can remove some wood next to the line to make room for a saw. (Fig. 4-13)

How do you keep the chisel perpendicular to the work? One of the best ways to do this is to make sure you're in a position to see what perpendicular is. (Fig. 4-14) This doesn't mean moving away from the work and sighting

A scribed line makes a great start to a joint.

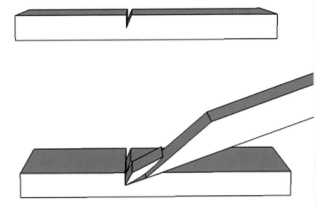

Paring out a chip up to the scribed line makes it easier to preserve that line. This can make sawing or additional chisel work more accurate.

Fig. 4-13

Fig. 4-14 - Oops. Chopping a mortise in this position (the workpiece is oriented from side to side in front of me) means I can't really see that I'm holding the chisel out of square to the work.

square; you won't be in a position to make the cut. Instead, you should sight down the edge of the chisel with your dominant eye. We all have a clear sense of square (think about how easy it is to notice a crooked picture hanging on the wall). The hard part is remembering to position either yourself or the work so you can see square. (Fig. 4-15) In some situations, it may be helpful to have a square on your bench as a reference. Some people also set up a mirror on the bench so they can check from a different perspective. Most important is that you need to be in the right position to see both the chisel and the square, yet remain able to make the cut in a controlled way. And often, you can use a previous cut as a reference.

How do you cut a line that is longer than the chisel without going over it at any point? First you need to prepare by cutting back close to the line; typically less than $1/32$" away. In harder woods, you may have to get even closer. The goal is to have just one easy paring cut remaining to get to the line. Then, start at one end, place the chisel's edge in the scribed line (bevel facing the waste side) and carefully pare down. (Fig. 4-17) Move the chisel along the line, registering the bulk of the tool off the cut you just made. Cut with only the leading eighth or quarter of the chisel, while the rest is held tight to the existing cut. In order to do this, you'll need to angle the chisel just a bit (sideways), with the leading edge higher up than the part registering off of the previous cut. (Fig. 4-18) You can move along a line quickly this way, and the results are, with

Fig. 4-15 - Here, I'm in a good position to see that the chisel lines up with the square.

Fig. 4-17 - Make sure you're not removing much wood when you put the chisel in the scribed line for your first paring cut.

Fig. 4-18 - Register the back of the chisel against the just-cut surface, and pare a little bit more away.

practice, amazingly accurate. Keep your upper body position stable as you move along, relying on your weight and larger muscle groups to push the chisel through the wood.

Bevel Up vs. Bevel Down

Most of the time you'll use the chisel with the bevel either facing up or towards the waste side of the cut. This is a matter of control. You need to know where the chisel is going to go during the cut. If the bevel is pushing the waste away, the back of the chisel should go straight in line with the direction of force. This is much less clear with the bevel down, because the direction of force is at an angle to the direction of the chisel in the cut.

There are times when putting the bevel down will give you access to something you couldn't get to any other way. (Fig. 4-19) At other times, you can use the bevel as something of a fulcrum to lever waste out of the way. Just be aware that prying with a chisel can fracture a sharp edge.

Oh, and for prying up carpet tacks: First, go to a garage sale and pick up a dirt-cheap old chisel; preferably one that looks like it's done plenty that kind of work before. Sharpen if necessary on a smooth concrete sidewalk. Then have at those tacks. The bevel should face down for good leverage.

Fig. 4-19 - You can clean out corners accurately and easily with the bevel of the chisel facing down.

Handplanes

Planes are probably the source of both the most frustration and the most pleasure in all of woodworking. Frustration, because until you're able to bring together an understanding of the tool, sharpening, technique and wood behavior, a plane may seem like an instrument uniquely suited for torturing wood. Once you do manage to bring these elements together, though, the plane is a tool that can do amazing things. Almost everyone marvels at the glassy smoothness of a well-planed surface or edge, and delights in making and showing off the translucent, gauzy shavings that are the plane's "waste product." It's not all about the sensual stuff, though. A plane is usually the fastest way to smooth a board. Luckily, it doesn't take as much as you might fear to get to that point.

The plane at its most basic is a sophisticated way to hold a blade. This enables cutting in ways that would otherwise be impossible. Just try to flatten a board, or to remove a 6'-long, $^1/_{1000}$"-thick shaving with a chisel. It's not that the cutting action is any different. It's still a sharp wedge and it still interacts with the wood in exactly the same way. But the specifics of how a blade is held allow the plane to do things well beyond what a chisel can do.

Crucial Factors in Cut Quality

Despite the staggering variety of plane types and sizes, successful planes all have certain common features that affect how well they cut. First, of course, is a sharp blade. But a sharp blade is not by itself enough to guarantee that a plane will cut well. The blade needs to be held securely. Not only does that blade need to stay exactly in position as it cuts the wood, but vibration and chatter during the cut, which can be significant problems, need to be kept to a minimum. This means carefully flattened surfaces on the parts of the plane that contact the blade (and on the blade itself). The more contact there is between the blade and the plane body the better. In addition, bench planes usually have a chip-breaker (sometimes called a cap iron, which can be confusing, because the lever-cap is also sometimes called a cap iron). Typically bolted to the plane iron, the chip-breaker (which only actually breaks chips if the plane is set for a coarser cut) adds additional rigidity to the blade, and dampens vibration right where the blade needs it most: out close to the edge. This area is otherwise unsupported. The chip-breaker should contact the blade securely and with no gaps. You may have to flatten or straighten out its leading edge to get this perfect contact.

Fig. 4-20 - This chip-breaker is twisted, and is useless until it's straightened out and has full contact with the back of the blade.

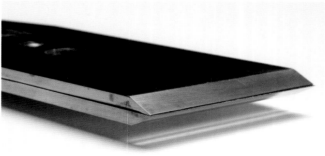

Fig. 4-21 - This chip-breaker is much more substantial, and is much better made. The contact with the back of the blade is tight all the way across.

Above is a range of bench planes, from a No. 7 at left, down to a No. 2 at right.

At right are a low-angle jack, a low-angle smoother and three block planes.

(Fig. 4-20 & 4-21) Changing to a better chip-breaker is a significant upgrade for many older or lesser-quality planes. It can improve performance significantly – at least as much as changing to a better blade.

There are a few other things that affect the quality of the plane. The plane's mouth should be adjusted according to the type of work that the plane will be doing. The tighter the mouth opening (the closer the front of the mouth is to the blade) the more the front of the plane can hold the wood fibers down in place just before the cut. This can help reduce tear-out. This is fine if you're mostly doing very fine work with the plane. But if you're looking to remove a lot of wood in a hurry, you will want to open up the mouth so that thicker shavings can easily pass through without clogging. This is not an adjustment you'll want to make often on a bench plane, where it means moving the frog forward or back. But it is easy to adjust the opening on a bevel-up plane that has an adjustable mouth; typically that involves simply loosening a knob, sliding a lever and then re-tightening the knob.

The sole of the plane needs to be relatively flat as well. This is really the reference surface for the blade as it moves across the wood, and it is difficult to control a plane with a distorted sole. But the entire sole doesn't need to be dead flat. The important parts are the periphery and the area all around the mouth.

We tend to think of cast iron as a very rigid and fixed material, but in truth, it does distort some under tension. If you need to flatten the sole of the plane (easily done with sandpaper on a glass, granite or a flat cast iron surface), you should do it with the plane iron in place, but backed out far enough that the blade edge is not at risk of being ruined at the same time.

Interestingly, the type (or lack) of an adjustment mechanism for blade depth is more a matter of convenience than of function or quality. Many top-quality planes have no mechanical means of adjustment; they can be adjusted by tapping the blade or the body of the plane with a mallet or small hammer. More common are adjustment mechanisms that use a knob for depth control, along with a lever for lateral adjustments to keep the blade straight. Some mechanisms combine the knob and lever into one.

Bench Planes and Block Planes

There are two main categories of planes: bench planes and block planes. These can be distinguished by their most notable difference: bench planes work with blades set with the bevel toward the bottom of the plane, where-

Differences Between Bench Planes and Block Planes

The bevel faces down on bench planes, and faces up on block planes. The bevel up plane has a bed machined into the sole of the tool. The bench plane has a separate, adjustable frog, which supports the blade and holds it at a specific angle. The block plane bed is machined to a much lower angle (12 or 20 degrees) than the typical bench plane frog (45, or less commonly, 50 or 55 degrees). But with the difference in blade orientation, the effective cutting angle is not always different.

The frog on a bench plane usually adjusts (with some fussing) forward and back, to control the size of the mouth opening in front of the plane iron. The block plane may have an adjustable mouth, where the front of the plane can be adjusted to control the same characteristic. The block plane does not have a chip-breaker. Not every bench plane does, although the vast majority certainly do.

The low-angle smoother has a bevel-up blade, a machined bed, and an adjustable mouth. The smoothing plane has a separate frog (in this case, a higher-angle one), and a chip-breaker.

as block planes have their bevels facing up. Why does that matter? In many respects, it doesn't matter at all. As far as the wood is concerned, all that matters is the angle of the blade. And it's not really the blade itself, but rather the effective angle: the angle at the very edge of the tool relative to the wood. Based on appearances, bench planes have a much higher blade angle. But block plane irons sit with the bevel facing up, so the effective cutting angle is the bed angle (the angle machined into the base of the tool on which the plane iron rests) plus the bevel angle. The main difference is much less than it appears. The normal blade angle for a bench plane is 45°, and this is then the effective cutting angle. Block planes are available with two common bed angles; 20° is considered standard, and 12° is called "low angle." But to this you need to add the bevel angle, because it faces up, so the effective angles are 45° (the same as a bench plane) or 37°, a little lower. The lower angle does make cutting end grain a little easier, because it is more likely to slice and less prone to compress the fibers.

Why bother with the block planes at all? Aside from the advantage of the lower cutting angle on end grain, small block planes are certainly easier to handle in situations

where you have to work vertically or with just one hand on a piece. Block planes are also less complicated in construction. But the real advantage lies in the ability to customize the effective cutting angle simply and easily by sharpening the blade at a different angle. If you encounter wood grain that is prone to tear-out, you can simply sharpen the blade at a steeper angle, or switch to a second blade sharpened at a steeper angle. The steeper the blade angle, the less likely it will tear out fibers.

Bench planes are more limited when it comes to changing the blade angle. Some makers offer higher frog angles as an option. Other than that, adding a "back bevel" to the blade is the only other possibility. Make sure that the back bevel doesn't interfere with good contact from the chip-breaker. And when sharpening the blade, you'll need to be able to find the same back bevel angle consistently when you remove the burr (see the chapter 5 for more on this). But back bevels do provide a relatively easy way to add to the effective cutting angle.

Straight vs. Crowned Blades

Most people sharpen plane irons with a straight edge and leave it at that. Some people knock the corners off the blade, so the plane iron won't leave small ridges (also known as plane tracks) at either side when planing a surface. And still others "crown," or curve the entire edge to some degree. An extreme example of the crowned blade is the scrub plane. (Fig. 4-22) This is a plane that is designed to remove a great deal of wood quickly when first working a rough board down to flat. The scrub plane has a narrow iron with a significant crown (my 1$^7/_{16}$" wide blade has a $^3/_{32}$" crown), and that helps remove wood in a hurry without bogging down in the cut. But a subtler crown can be useful, too. A smoothing plane with a very slight crown that bellies out just a few thousandths of an inch won't leave tracks (the cut will feather out to nothing at the sides), but will instead have a subtly varied surface that tells the story of the hand-work that went into cutting it. (Fig. 4-23)

The crown is also useful for squaring edges on boards. Shifting the plane over to one side or the other means that the crowned blade will cut off center, and will cut deeper on one side of the edge than the other. This is a good way to adjust an edge back to square a few thousandths of an inch at a time. (Fig. 4-24) But you can do a similar trick with a straight plane iron. (Fig. 4-25)

Sharpening a crowned edge is definitely harder than simply sharpening a straight edge. Consider it an option to explore once you're completely comfortable with both your

Fig. 4-22 - The pronounced crown of the scrub plane blade helps you to remove a lot of wood in a hurry. The results aren't necessarily pretty, but that's not the point.

sharpening and your planing techniques.

Plane Set-up

Sharpening the plane iron is only the beginning of getting a well-tuned plane ready to use. The plane iron needs to be installed in the plane and adjusted for the type of cut you want to make. You'll need to make some test cuts to get all of the adjustments just right, so keep a piece of scrap wood handy.

With bench planes, you have to bolt the chip-breaker

Fig. 4-23 - The very subtle crowning of this smoothing plane iron means that the cut will feather out to nothing at either edge.

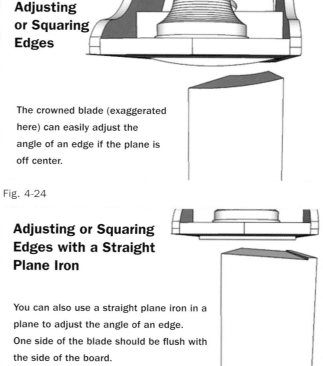

Adjusting or Squaring Edges

The crowned blade (exaggerated here) can easily adjust the angle of an edge if the plane is off center.

Fig. 4-24

Adjusting or Squaring Edges with a Straight Plane Iron

You can also use a straight plane iron in a plane to adjust the angle of an edge. One side of the blade should be flush with the side of the board.

Fig. 4-25

to the blade first. You don't want to drag the chip-breaker across your freshly sharpened edge, so slip the blade onto the chip-breaker cross-wise, and well away from the edge. Rotate the blade, and then slide the chip-breaker up toward the edge. Set it about $^{1}/_{64}$" to $^{1}/_{32}$" back from the edge, and tighten the bolt carefully (the blade will sometimes move) and securely.

Carefully insert this assembly into the plane, being careful not to damage your sharp edge on the plane body. Slip the slot in the chip-breaker over the tab in the adjustment mechanism, add the lever cap and clamp the blade in place.

On block planes, you simply insert the blade (bevel facing up), registering the adjustment slot over the adjustment mechanism and lock it down with the cap iron.

How tight should the cap iron or lever cap be? Tight enough to hold the blade securely in place while still being loose enough to be able to adjust it without much effort. You shouldn't be able to push the plane iron around at all with just your fingers, but the knob and lever should work well.

Preliminary adjustments can be made by feel. Turn the plane over and check the blade projection. Adjust it so that you can just feel the blade beyond the sole of the plane. Straighten out any obvious skewing of the blade. Many block planes don't have a mechanism for correcting this skew; you can either tap on the side of the iron with a small mallet or hammer, or loosen the cap iron and push the blade straight with your fingers.

The plane needs to be set so the plane iron cuts perfectly straight and square (which is parallel to the plane's sole). The best way to do this is do a series of test cuts on a scrap of wood. From this point on, every adjustment should be based on results. No cut? Adjust deeper. A deep

Fig. 4-26 - A shaving only on one side (here, on the left) means the plane iron needs to be adjusted.

cut? Back the plane iron out a little. Eventually what you need to examine is how evenly the two sides of the blade are cutting. Offset the plane from one side to the other and look at the shavings. It's very rare to get even shavings by chance. The easiest way to correct this is to back the blade off until it's only cutting on one side or the other. (Fig. 4-26) Then straighten out the blade just a little and test again. You may find that the blade doesn't cut at all any more. That's a sign that you've straightened things out a bit. Advance the blade a little bit, and check again. Keep making these little adjustments until you get a very fine, even shaving all the way across the blade. (Fig. 4-27) This will mean the blade is set up square. Now you can adjust to whatever depth you need for your work. This process seems slow at first, but as you get a feel for what you're after and for what the various adjustments accomplish, you'll learn to do this quickly and easily.

Fig. 4-27 - Ahh!

Sharpening Issues Unrelated to Sharpness

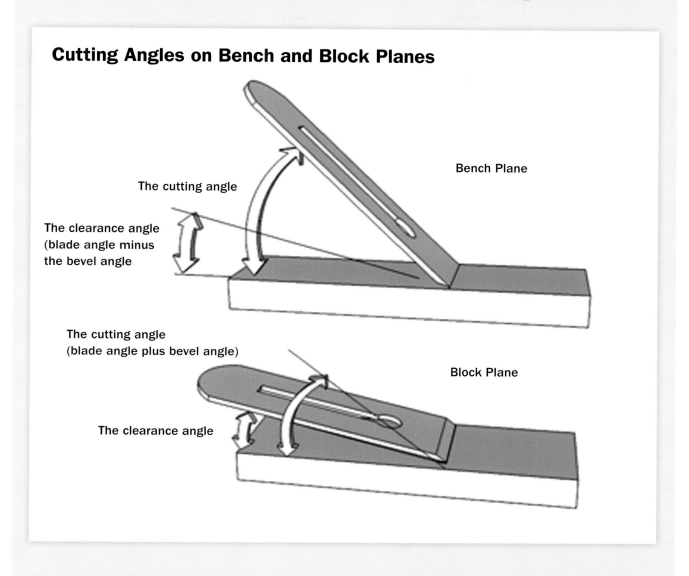

Cutting Angles on Bench and Block Planes

The cutting angle

Bench Plane

The clearance angle
(blade angle minus
the bevel angle

The cutting angle
(blade angle plus bevel angle)

Block Plane

The clearance angle

The effective cutting angle changes a number of characteristics of a plane. The steeper the angle, the less likely it is to cause tear-out. But steeper angles are harder to push through the wood. And you'll find that as the angle gets steeper, the quality of the surface left behind changes as well. At higher angles (steeper than 55°), the wood fibers tend to be smashed off rather than sliced off. The resulting surface is not quite as smooth as a sliced cut

The clearance angle is the angle on the bottom of the blade. This varies with the bevel angle on a bench-style

plane, but is the same as the bed angle on a bevel-up plane. Although this is typically something that you can ignore, you might run into an issue if the bevel on a bench plane iron gets too steep. You'll need around 12° of clearance angle – anything less than that and the plane will start to give you trouble. To put this is more concrete terms, a bench plane iron sharpened at 25° with a 9° micro-bevel will run into trouble, as will a 28° primary bevel with a 6° micro-bevel.

Plane Technique

Planing is the embodiment of the principle that woodworking requires your all, from your fingers down to your toes. It requires good positioning and alignment, as well as good coordination between different types of movements.

Position your hands on both the knob and the tote so that both wrists are straight (a line drawn straight down your forearm should aim right between your thumb and forefinger, and extend straight to the center of the front knob of the plane. (Fig. 4-28) Your rear forearm should line up perfectly with the plane, with your elbow close to the body. (Fig. 4-29) Your front foot should start out with the toes roughly under the front of the plane. The rear foot should be back a little farther than the typical woodworking stance and angled at 45° to 60°. Both knees should be bent, and the hips pressed a bit forward.

Hold the front of the plane firmly down on the board – most of the pressure should be on your front hand – with the blade not yet touching the end of the board. (Fig. 4-30) Start your body moving first. Your front foot should slide or step forward, moving your hips forward. This is like a slow lunge. As soon as your rear elbow is a couple of inches behind your hip, you should start pushing the plane forward (In other words, your body actually starts in motion just a tiny bit before you move the plane). You should feel most of this push as coming from the back foot. If you don't get that feeling, try slowing the process down. The slower you go, the more you'll need to push from your back foot. And this is how it should feel at normal speed as well. Continue

Fig. 4-28 - In the basic position for planing, the right forearm is lined up perfectly with the plane.

to slide the front foot forward as you plane forward. The total movement should be roughly the equivalent of a large step forward. You don't want to extend that front foot so far that you're off balance, though. At the end of the cut, your arms will extend forward from the shoulders to push the plane farther. (Fig. 4-31)

Longer boards are not much harder. If you're taking a light cut on a thinner board, you might actually be able to walk the plane forward. But on most long boards, it can be better to stop planing, maintain pressure with both hands on the plane, shift your feet forward, then re-start the

Fig. 4-29 - Starting to plane.

Fig. 4-30 - My body starts to move forward (left foot slides forward), but the plane hasn't moved yet.

Fig. 4-31 - Now I've pushed the plane forward. Note the my right elbow (not visible) is still not all that far from my hip. You can see how much of a push comes from the back foot.

planing motion. With just a bit of practice, you should be able to do this without breaking the shaving or leaving any evidence that you stopped the cut on the board.

Whatever the length of the board, as you get to the far end, you need to transfer most of the downward pressure to your rear hand. This helps counteract the natural tendency to either over-cut or fall off the end of the board. Some people describe this as feeling as if you're trying to hollow out the middle of the board.

As usual, there is a separation of force and control. Most of the time, the power behind the plane comes from the lower body, all the way down to the toes. The planing mo-

tion is almost like a lunge in fencing. There is, of course, upper body movement as well, and you can work more with your upper body on very short pieces. But if you rely solely on throwing your arms forward to generate the bulk of the movement, you won't have much control. You'll also get really tired.

Planing requires a very dynamic control over pressure. This is mostly a matter of balancing pressure between your hands and arms. You can't just slide the tool forward over the work and expect to see good results. Start the cut with more pressure on the front of the plane, and then transition to more pressure on the back as you work along the

Core Planing

Planing involves the whole body, and a fair bit of movement. But overall, it should still feel "contained." By that, I mean that most of the upper-body work takes place fairly close to the body, which is where you have the most control. The elbow on your pushing arm doesn't get very far from your hip. The farther from your core that you work, the more difficult it will be to control balance and pressure on the plane.

Skewing a Plane

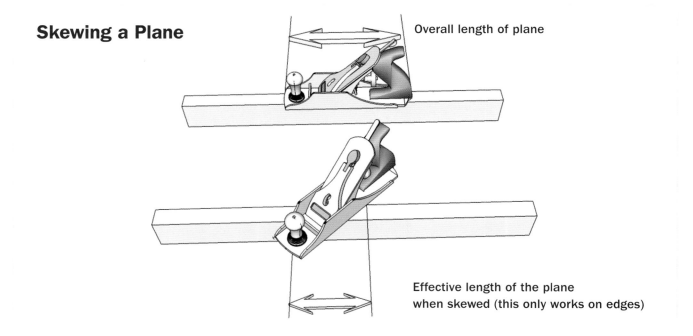

Overall length of plane

Effective length of the plane
when skewed (this only works on edges)

Fig. 4-32

board. Most people have trouble at the start of the cut. This is usually the case of not enough downward pressure with the front hand, and starting the forward movement with too much upper body involvement.

When you're first learning to plane, you should keep the tool aligned straight with the board you're planing. As you get better control over the pressure balance between hands, you can start experimenting with skewed cuts. These can offer some advantages, but come with potential disadvantages as well. The main advantage is that skewing the plane creates more of a slicing cut. Think of the difference between just pushing a knife down on a piece of meat as opposed to slicing the knife through; the latter is definitely easier. Skewing the plane also effectively lowers

Fig. 4-33 - Be sure to watch for evidence of planing out of square. You can see this on the top leg. The leg on the bottom is still square across.

the cutting angle of the blade a little. This is similar to how traversing up a steep hill on a bicycle actually makes the climb less steep than going straight up. Although a lower angle might normally cause more tear-out in difficult grain, the slicing action seems to be more significant and counteracts this tendency. Skewing a plane on a narrower board also effectively shortens up the sole of the plane, which can allow you get into low spots (or even gentle curves) that you might not otherwise be able to plane. (Fig. 4-32)

Staying square to an edge when planing is very much a matter of practice, but there is technique involved as well. The more you understand how to go about correcting an edge that is out of square, the easier it is to get back to where you want to be.

Poor tool set-up is the most common reason for an edge going out of square. If the blade is skewed, each stroke will remove more material from one side than the other. This quickly adds up. So the first rule for staying square is to be sure your plane is set properly. Each time you pick up the tool you should quickly check to see if it is cutting an even shaving all the way across. Planes do go out of adjustment (especially if the cap iron is a little bit loose). Keep an eye on your shavings to be sure they stay even across the edge all throughout the planing process.

If your blade is straight and you're still planing an edge out of square, you need to concentrate on technique. Holding the plane square is a learned skill, not a trick. You should feel the sole of the plane solidly on the edge throughout the entire stroke. Concentrate on how the plane feels on the edge, and on planing straight and well-

Fig. 4-34 - The fingers of my left hand help me register the side of the plane flush with the edge of the board.

Fig. 4-35 - Alignment on a pull stroke is very similar. But the grips and the movement are different. You still want to use your whole body.

centered. As the rest of your technique comes together and you get a better feel for the tool (and staying contained as you use it), this will start to come more naturally.

One way to help learn faster is to check your results more often. It won't do you much good to plane an edge for 5 minutes only to discover you've planed it to an 85° angle. Check with a square every few strokes so you can correct any tendency to lean before it becomes a major problem.

Watch what you're doing as you plane as well. If you're smoothing out a machined surface, you'll notice a difference between the original machined surface (table-sawn, jointed, planed, routed or band-sawn) and the smoother and shinier planed areas. Watch the in-

Fig. 4-36 - Balancing a plane on a narrow edge is easier if you lower your hands on the plane.

terface carefully. If the machined edge was reliably square to start, you'll stay square if you remove the machine marks evenly across the board. (Fig. 4-33)

It's easy to correct an out-of-square edge, even without a crowned blade. (Fig. 4-23) Just move the plane over far enough so that the edge of the plane is flush with the edge of the board. (Fig. 4-34) Because the plane iron does not extend all the way to the edge, the blade can't cut there, but it will cut the rest of the board.

This can be repeated as much as necessary. You will need to take one or more additional passes with the plane centered on the board to eliminate the extra facet on the face that the offset planing creates.

Just because planes are built with handles that invite a certain grip doesn't mean that you can't hold a plane in

other ways. So long as you can maintain the necessary control while you push or pull the tool, any number of other grips will work.

Japanese planes are designed for pulling, and there's no reason you can't pull on a western-style bench or block plane. Some of the alignment is a little different, but alignment and separation of force and control are still important. Most of the pulling force should come from the lower body. Arm alignment tends to come more naturally on a pull than in a push; the forearm of the front hand should line up with the plane and the direction of cut. (Fig. 4-35)

You may want to try a different plane grip when planing a narrow edge (with a push stroke). The key here is to shift your grip lower on the plane. You'll be closer to the bottom of the plane, so you won't have as much leverage to tip the plane on the edge and will have a better feel for flat on the edge. Place the thumb of your front hand directly in front of the knob, on the plane bed. Grip the handle in back as low as possible on the handle without interfering with the wood. This should feel more secure on the edge. (Fig. 4-36)

You can also change a normal grip slightly to give you a reference for aligning one side of the plane with the edge of a board. Just drop your forefinger, middle finger and ring finger to the side of the plane, instead of wrapping them around either the tote, frog or knob. (See Fig. 4-34 on previous page.)

A plane can be used with one hand, but it does take practice. You're asking the one hand to both push and guide the plane, combining force and control. Smaller planes are certainly easier for one-handed use, with block planes being the most suitable. (Fig. 4-37)

The most common one-handed use for a larger plane is in conjunction with a shooting board. This will often require gripping the plane in the middle so you can keep a good balance of pressure between front and back. Special handles are also available that can help with this grip. (Fig. 4-38)

Planing Across the Grain
Most of the time, you'll plane with the grain.

Fig. 4-37 - It's easy to use a block plane with one hand, although you can also use two hands when necessary.

Fig. 4-38 - One-hand planing is also called for with a shooting board. You'll have to figure out a comfortable grip that offers the necessary control on your plane.

And this is necessary for smoothing. But flattening a board or a panel calls for planing in multiple directions. Flattening usually starts with cutting directly across the grain. This peels up the fibers rather than slicing them. You can improve the cross-grain cuts by skewing the plane 25 to 35 degrees (but still pushing at 90 degrees to the grain direction). This helps the plane to slice the fibers instead of just plowing them up, and usually leaves a better surface.

The one very real problem with planing across the grain is that the back edge of the wood will tend to split off. The terrifically descriptive word for this is spelching. Chamfer the back edge, clamp another board back there to support the fibers at the edge, or plan on ripping the spelched wood off after the flattening is done. (Fig. 4-39)

Planing End Grain

Planing end grain is really no different that chiseling end grain, but it's easier to do successfully. You can't plane all the way across a board; you'll blow out fibers at the end of the cut. (Fig. 4-40) But end grain does not have a "direction" like long grain does. So you can plane part way across a board, then turn it around and plane back. A sharp plane iron is a must if you're going to avoid compressing the end-grain fibers and breaking them away from their neighbors. And a lower effective cutting angle will help as well – although a very sharp bench plane does just fine.

You can also wet the end grain with either water or mineral spirits (which won't raise the grain) to help plane end grain more easily.

Fig. 4-39 - Just a bit of spelching.

Fig. 4-40 - Splitting off the back is a fact of life when planing end-grain.

Marking Knives and Gauges

Marking knives and Gauges are important companions for many different hand tools. A scored line can give you exact chisel placement, as well as the actual finished edge of a joint. When planing a board to a thickness that has been scored with a marking gauge, you can see a feather-edge when you get close to your line. (Fig. 4-41)

But marking knives and marking gauges can also improve machine work. The crisp, unambiguous lines help in all of your work, and the repeatability of marking gauges also means that lines

Fig. 4-41 - This edge was scribed (on the edge) for thickness, and planing down to the scribed line creates the feather edge visible on this board.

The Micro-bevel on a Marking Knife

Fig. 4-42

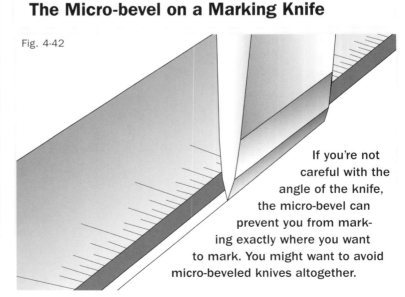

If you're not careful with the angle of the knife, the micro-bevel can prevent you from marking exactly where you want to mark. You might want to avoid micro-beveled knives altogether.

Sharpening the Marking Knife

Slightly rounding over the sharp point on a marking knife makes it easier to use.

Fig. 4-44

Fig. 4-43 - Marking gauges can have knives (back left), points (right) or scribing disks (front).

can be accrately marked over and over again. There's more discussion on this in the chapter on layout, but it's important to understand how to use these tools properly to get the best results.

Everyone seems to develop his or her own preference in marking knives, from X-Acto knives to fancy custom knives. They're all designed to do the same simple thing: scribe a clear and precise line in the wood. The main distinction is between knives with a flat back and the bevel on just one side, or those with bevels on both sides with both sides tapering equally toward the edge. The former work very well when laying out against a thin straightedge, where it's easy to hold the knife with the flat side against your reference and still hold the tool square to the work. Double-bevel knives may be easier to use if you're scribing off of another part, which might get in the way of holding the tool square. Just hold one of the bevels flat against the reference. Note that either of these two types can be sharpened with a micro-bevel. This can be a problem with the double-bevel knives, because the scribed line will be offset from the face of both primary bevels, and it may be hard to place the mark exactly where you need it. (Fig. 4-42)

Marking gauges fall into a few different categories: gauges with scribing knives (both straight knives and cutting disks); gauges with scribing points; and even gauges with pencils. (Fig. 4-43) The scribing knives are probably the most useful, because they will cut cleanly either with or across the grain. Straight scribing knives should be sharpened carefully, and seem to work best with a very small radius at the tip. (Fig. 4-44) The scribing disks vary in how effectively they cut, with more acute angles working better than the blunter angles. The disks can be sharpened without too much trouble. Remove the disk from the gauge, and then hone the flat side on a series of sharpening stones or fine sandpapers.

Scribing points are traditional on mortise gauges. These have pairs of points that are either adjustable in relation to one another, or are set a fixed distance apart (generally, the distance is the same as the width of a specific mortise chisel). Scribing points do not work well across the grain; they tear wood fibers rather than cut them cleanly. (Fig. 4-45) But they do work with the grain, which is how you lay out both mortises and tenons. The lines from scribing points may be slightly less precise than those from scribing knives. This is because the points score a line with bevels on both sides of the line, whereas knives leave one vertical cut. But for cutting mortise-and-tenon joints, the lines made by the points work well enough. Think of the bevels

Fig. 4-45 - Points leave fuzzy lines across the grain.

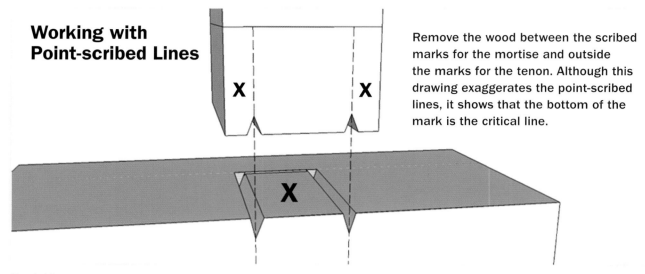

Working with Point-scribed Lines

Remove the wood between the scribed marks for the mortise and outside the marks for the tenon. Although this drawing exaggerates the point-scribed lines, it shows that the bottom of the mark is the critical line.

X X

X

Fig. 4-46

on both sides of the line as the walls of a canyon. Cut away the appropriate wall of the canyon down to the bottom in each case and you've got a well-fit joint. (Fig. 4-46)

Pencil gauges are good for rough layout, and leave easily visible (and easily erased) lines, but are generally not as precise (or at least without incessant sharpening) as either knife or point-based gauges.

Using a Marking Gauge

Marking gauges appear simple to use, but they can still pose plenty of challenges. It's not easy to hold the gauge tight against the end of a board while you scribe.

Start by bracing the board you're scribing against a bench dog or stop. This way you don't have to concentrate on holding the work in place against the force of the other hand. Grip the marking gauge so that you've got your thumb and middle finger or forefinger just behind the

fence. Most of the pressure as you make the cut should go toward holding the fence securely against the end of the board you're scribing. Concentrate more on this than on cutting the line and you're less likely to go astray. Downward pressure is only a secondary concern.

Make sure you pull the tool toward your body. Your elbow and shoulder act as pivot points, and if you push away from yourself, the natural tendency will be to move your hand away from the wood. You could certainly overcome this, but it's not worth it. Pulling is easy, and the pivoting motion of the lower arm tends to tighten the tool against the wood. (Fig. 4-47)

With a scribing knife or point(s), it helps to angle the tool forward in the direction of the cut. This tips the point or knife a little off vertical and usually makes for a cleaner cut. This isn't necessary (because nothing will change) with a scribing disk. (Fig. 4-48)

Fig. 4-47 - Pull the marking gauge. The natural pivot of your shoulder will push it tighter to the end of the board.

Fig. 4-48 - Tilting the gauge toward you as you pull usually makes for a cleaner cut.

Scrapers

Card scrapers are still thought of as the professional's secret weapon. They are probably the cheapest good tools you can buy (you can afford top-quality scrapers on almost any budget), and they can smooth a surface regardless of grain direction problems. Why are they regarded as a secret? It's probably because the sharpening process appears mysterious and hard to master. But it just takes a little bit of know-how and practice to master forming a burr, and a little more to get the feel of the actual cut.

One thing that is mysterious about card scrapers is their name; they don't actually "scrape" the wood. A true scraping action compresses the fibers into failure (it just smashes them off). This is how a scraper without a burr (and a sharp edge) actually functions. But the burr on a typical scraper is indeed a cutting edge, and it cuts more like a plane iron. It's a microscopically small edge, and the body of the scraper doesn't allow that edge to get very far in lifting up fibers, so it is still a terrific tool for woods that are difficult to plane.

To create the burr on the edge of a scraper you need to "turn" the edge of the tool with a burnisher. This burr is fairly fragile, and doesn't last all that long, but each card scraper has four edges that can be used, and you can also use more of the edge than just the center by shifting your hands to one side or the other.

Sharpening Scrapers

Sharpening a scraper is really a combination of sharpening and then deforming the metal into an edge that will work for you. This is a multi-step process that may seem unusually complex as you get started. Once you're familiar with the steps, it's both quick and simple to do.

You start by filing, or 'jointing' the edge. The best file for the task is a 6" mill bastard file, something you should be able to find at a good hardware store. Fit a handle to the file to make it easier to hold, and for safety (the tang of a file can poke you pretty badly). The filing is mostly to remove any previous burrs or work-hardened steel (the burnishing at the end of the process hardens the steel somewhat and makes forming another burr impossible). Clamp the scraper upright in a vise, sticking up about an inch above the bench surface. Hold the file square to the scraper with the handle in your left hand and push for-

Fig. 4-49 - Jointing the edge of a scraper freehand with a file.

Fig. 4-50 - This is an incredibly simple jig for holding a file for jointing the edge of a scraper. Just hold the wood tight to the face of the scraper as you push the file forward.

ward. (Fig. 4-49) You may notice that the file doesn't quite cut the steel at first; the edge has been work-hardened by previous burnishing and resists a little. Continue filing until you feel the file cutting along the full length of the edge. Keeping the file exactly at 90° is a challenge, but it is possible to get it right by hand if you register the back of your hand on the benchtop as you slide forward to file. Confine most of the forward movement to your lower body.

Some companies sell special jigs or guides that will help you file at 90° to the edge. It's also easy to make your own guide by cutting a dado in a block of wood. Push a file that you've set up this way straight along the edge. (Fig. 4-50)

The next step is to "stone" the edge. The file leaves a surface that's a little too rough and creates the wrong kind of burr, so you want to refine it a little on either a diamond stone or on some very fine sandpaper on a flat, hard surface. Taking the edge to a finer grit works just like it does with a chisel or plane, and gives you a more durable edge. A wooden guide block (a good one is 1½" square by 8"-10" long) can help you keep the edge perfectly square while stoning it. Just put the guide block on the abrasive and hold the scraper against the side as you run it back and forth along the abrasive. You'll want to move the block and scraper around on the abrasive surface to avoid excessive wear on such a narrow area. (Fig. 4-51)

Then lay the scraper flat on the abrasive and rub once or twice to remove any burr and square up the edge. You should have a crisp, clean corner along each of the edges. If there's any rounding over of the edge, you should start over and re-file; you won't be able to make the scraper work.

Now it's time to actually "turn" the burr. You'll need a

Fig. 4-51 - Here, I'm stoning the edge of the scraper. Keep the scraper and the wood block moving around on the stone.

burnisher for this. The burnisher is a hardened steel rod – sometimes with a handle or contained in a jig – that's necessary to create the burr on the edge of the scraper.

If you're working with a simple burnisher, start with the scraper flat on a workbench, about ¾" away from the edge of the bench. Lay the burnisher down flat on the scraper, and then rub it across the face of the scraper a few times. (Fig. 4-52) Then tip the handle of the burnisher down a bit (the bench will keep you from tipping too much) and rub a few more times at this slight angle. It really doesn't take all that much pressure (about as much as you might use to spread peanut butter on bread), and four to six passes should be enough.

Some people use a bit of oil to lubricate the steel while burnishing. This is fine, but by no means necessary. Tage Frid used to talk about using "nose oil"; he would rub his thumb along the side of his nose, then swipe his thumb (carefully) along the edge before burnishing. That works, but then again, so does not using any oil at all.

Move the scraper out over the edge of the workbench. Hold the burnisher vertically in your hand with your thumb positioned to apply pressure (to the burnisher) against the narrow edge of the scraper. Pull toward you for three passes at 90° to the face of the scraper, then angle the top of the burnisher in about 5° (and only 5°), and make three more passes at this angle. (Fig. 4-53) Again: This does not take a great deal of pressure. You should be able to feel a very slight burr on the edge. Then flip the scraper around or over as needed and burnish each of the remaining three edges.

Burnishing jigs have their own instructions you can follow.

Using a Scraper

Scrapers can be pushed or pulled. What's most important is holding the tools at the proper angle, putting pressure right behind the edge and

Fig. 4-52 - The next step in burnishing a hook on the scraper is consolidating the edge.

Fig. 4-53 - And finally, burnish the actual hook.

then mostly relying on the lower body to push forward or pull back. As with a handplane, there is also some arm movement (mostly from the shoulders), but you're better off most of the time if you think about holding your upper body in position and pushing from the toes as you would with a plane.

The grip for pushing a scraper puts your thumbs together in the center of the bottom edge; they will touch on the wood when you're scraping. The forefingers wrap around the top, and the middle and ring fingers around the sides of the scraper. Spring the scraper slightly, pulling back on the sides. Your elbows should start out close to your body, just in front of your hips. Angle the scraper forward about 45°, push down slightly, then move your body forward. You may have to adjust the angle slightly, but you should feel the edge bite into the wood, and should produce a very fine shaving (not dust). Experiment as needed with pressure and angle until you get the feel of making shavings. (Fig. 4-54)

The grip for pulling may seem more natural. Just the thumbs stay on the front side of the scraper, and the other fingers all go to the back, forefingers touching in the middle, down by the edge. Spread your thumbs out; your elbows will move out from your body as well. Use your thumbs to spring the scraper slightly if desired (it offers more precise control), angle the blade 45° toward you and pull back. (Fig. 4-55 & 4-56) The lower body motion should be one of shifting your weight back to the back foot (your feet should be spread apart in the basic balanced position, of course).

With either grip, you'll have to pay attention to the side-to-side balance of pressure between your hands, especially on narrower edges. It's easy to push down too hard on one side of the edge of a board and rip up the corner

Fig. 4-54 - Pushing a scraper is as much a whole-body experience as planing. But it all starts with the grip.

Fig. 4-55 - Pulling the scraper is another option. Thumbs to the outside...

Fig. 4-56 - ...your other fingers toward the middle on the back of the scraper.

with a scraper; try this on a scrap board so you learn what to avoid.

You'll notice rather quickly that a scraper gets hot as you scrape, especially when pushing. There are some easy solutions. You can cut the thumbs off a pair of gloves and slip those on for scraping. Some woodworking catalogs have little leather and elastic finger protectors (usually listed with carving tools – they're missing the boat on these) if you don't want to make your own. Or you can stick a refrigerator magnet onto the scraper. The magnet will act as a good insulator and keep your thumbs from scorching, and can be easily removed for sharpening or when you switch to a different scraper. (Fig. 4-57)

Other Scraper Options

Card scrapers aren't the only options for scraping. There are a number of tools that can best be seen as a cross between a scraper and a handplane. These include scraper planes and cabinet scrapers. You can also use a low-angle, bevel-up plane with a blade that has been ground (or micro-beveled) at a very high angle, effectively creating a scraper plane. All of these options offer one major advantage: the ability to keep surfaces flat while they clean up the surface. You shouldn't turn to one of these first for flattening a board or panel, though. They are designed to remove little material, and usually require more pushing to do that work. The sharpening method for these tools is different, and usually involves actually sharpening the bevel at a 45° angle. Some people add a burr, but most of the time it's just the sharp edge that does the scraping. Sharpening a low-angle bevel-up plane iron at 75° to 90° is not something you want to try freehand, but commercial sharpening jigs won't be much help either. The solution is to use a block of wood cut at the desired angle as a guide while you sharpen. A burr here isn't necessary either, but you may want to try one if results are not what you're looking for. (Fig. 4-58)

The low-angle plane as a scraper plane may seem like an odd idea, but it has two advantages. It's much easier to

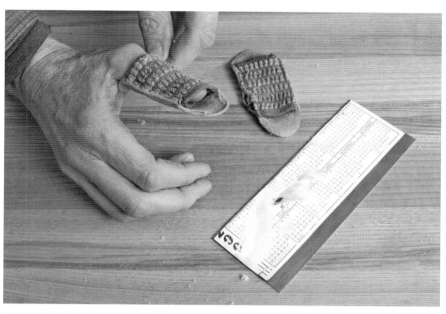

Fig. 4-57 - Scraping gets hot! Protect your fingers with either finger protectors or a refrigerator magnet.

Fig. 4-58 - I've moved my left hand out of the way to show you the block. It would be hard to sharpen like this.

adjust than any of the tools actually designed as scraper planes. And it's also better at eliminating vibration and chatter. That's because the effective thickness of the blade on a low-angle plane turned into a scraper is about 4", but the height is only about $\frac{1}{8}$". On a scraper plane, those di-

Fig. 4-59 - A chisel makes a good scraper, especially in areas where it's hard to use another tool.

mensions are reversed.

You can even use a chisel as a scraper from time to time. Hold it upright on the wood about 15° off of vertical. (Fig. 4-59) A pencil-type grip down near the edge with your other hand on the handle will help you support the tool as you pull it along the surface. You'll have to find the balance between downward pressure (not much) and pull until the tool cuts well.

Handsaws

Sawing wood is at the root of all woodworking. The process seems obvious enough – the teeth cut away the wood – but the fibrous nature of wood means it's really more complex than that. So how does a saw actually cut wood? The "bundle of straws" I first mentioned in chapter 1 can help explain the process.

Ripping

Cutting parallel to the length of the fibers is called ripping. A saw that is set up for ripping is designed to cut away small sections of the fibers that are easily separated from their neighbors on the sides.

The saw's teeth are oriented so the edges are perpendicular to the fibers in the wood. They are essentially like a

Ripsaw Teeth

The teeth on a ripsaw are filed straight across

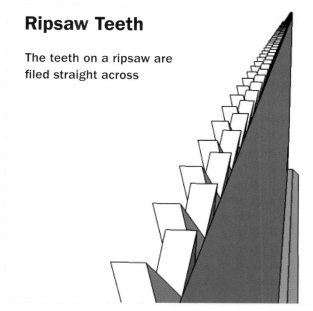

Fig. 4-60

Crosscut Saw Teeth

Crosscut saw teeth have sharp points that score the fibers cleanly before cutting them away

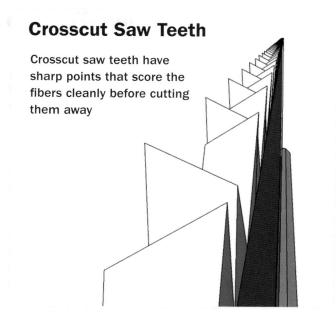

Fig. 4-61

row of chisels standing more or less upright. At this steep angle, the teeth most resemble scrapers. (Fig. 4-60) This set-up works well when either ripping (with the saw across the end grain, or cutting with the grain (with the saw flat on the surface and parallel to the direction of the fibers; not a common cut). This is because in both of these orientations the connection between the cut fibers and their neighbors to either side is weak and the separation will be clean at the sides of the cut.

Crosscutting

Fibers do not behave the same way when crosscut, which involves cutting crosswise through the grain (perpendicular to the fibers). Ripsaw teeth will easily roll fibers out of the way if used in this way, but these fibers extend in either direction from the intended cut. Because fibers are stronger than the connections between them, they will tear away from the sides of the cut, but not necessarily cleanly or where you want them to. In order to deal with this problem, crosscut saws have sharp points on the outside edges of the teeth that act like knives and slice the fibers cleanly before pushing the short, pre-sliced fibers out of the way. The bevels on the teeth that create these points alternate from tooth to tooth, so left and right pointed teeth follow each other all the way down the saw. (Fig. 4-61)

Crosscut saws tend to have fewer problems ripping than ripsaws do cutting across the grain. They're just slower at it. So crosscut saws are generally a little more versatile. It's not that ripsaws can't cut crosswise. It's that they can leave ragged edges.

The distinctions between rip and crosscut saws remain

true even when you add power into the equation. Table saw blades are surprisingly similar in tooth configuration to handsaws. Although there are dedicated rip and crosscut blades (as well as many other blades for special materials), there are blades that can both rip and crosscut effectively. These blades are closer to crosscut blades. They have pointed edges for scoring the fibers first, and often a third tooth type designed to clear out the waste quickly. They may not be quite as fast in a rip cut as a pure ripping blade, but they are still very effective.

Set

Most handsaws have one other important characteristic: the teeth are "set." The teeth are offset somewhat to both sides so that the kerf (the path that is cut by the blade) is actually wider than the body of the saw that will need to follow into the wood. This is a practical solution to the problem of friction. If there isn't enough room for the body of the saw (the sawplate) in the kerf, the saw will quickly bind in the cut, and that will get worse and worse as the cut gets deeper. The amount (and accuracy) of the set is one major factor in the quality of cut of which a saw is capable. There is another, much less common solution to the problem of friction, though. Some high-quality blades change the cross-section of the sawplate, so that the bottom of the blade (where the teeth are) is thicker than the rest of the saw. Some special saws that are designed specifically for cutting flush on a surface may have no set at all (or set only on the side of the saw that faces away from the surface). This keeps the saw teeth from scratching the surface during the cut, as would happen with a saw with set.

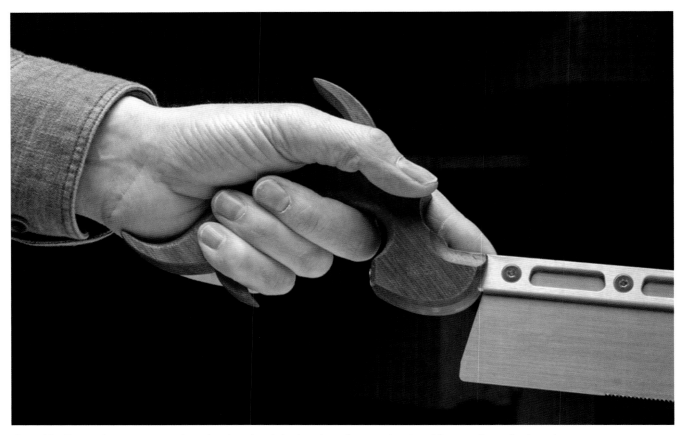

Fig. 4-62 - The basic grip on a handsaw is relaxed and designed to align your hand and forearm for optimal cutting.

Using Saws

It's hard to saw successfully with poor saw technique. Accuracy and quality of cut depend entirely on your input, and issues of alignment body position, and where the motion comes from are all critical.

Good saw technique starts with the grip, which helps set up the alignment process throughout your body. Start with three fingers (middle finger, ring finger and pinky) wrapped around the handle. Your forefinger should point straight forward and should rest alongside the spine of the saw. There's usually a little notch in the handle (on a good saw) that's designed just for this. The thumb should also point forward toward the end of the saw. (Fig. 4-62) As is true for so many other tools, a line drawn straight down your forearm should extend directly down the tool. (Fig. 4-63) This is the neutral wrist position. Pay particular attention to this. If your forearm doesn't line up, you'll have to compensate in both your wrist and your shoulder to keep the saw moving in a straight line. (Fig. 4-64) That's not impossible; it's just unlikely. Now it's time to set up the rest of your body.

Much of the rest of the body position should seem familiar by now; it's the basic woodworking stance once again. The foot opposite your sawing hand should be forward, close to the workbench. The other foot should be back, at least shoulder width, and angled at about 45°. Hips should also be at about 45° to the work. Your elbow should be able to just swing freely past your hip as you cut.

Most of the force for moving the saw should come from your shoulder. Other than pivoting at the elbow, the rest of your arm should just feel like a linkage, with no extraneous movement. (Fig. 4-65) The force is then transmitted through the heel of your hand directly to the saw. Your grip should remain relaxed – gripping harder only adds tension, not control.

When all of your movements are lined up properly (and you've had a chance to practice), you should be able to move the saw back and forth smoothly. Practice this motion, and pay attention to moving the back of the saw in a straight line. You should imagine that it's moving back and forth as if on rails, with no side-to-side wobble.

Starting the Cut

There's no question that starting a rip cut is the hardest part of sawing for a beginner. It often seems that there's nothing you can do other than to drag the saw backward. And this often cuts a rutted kerf that actually causes even more trouble getting started, because more teeth are trapped in these ruts.

It's generally easier to start the cut on a corner of the

Fig. 4-63 - Good alignment is the key to accurate sawing. I use the back of my fingernail to help place the saw where it needs to go.

Fig. 4-64 - Poor alignment adds extra movement and is much harder to control.

Fig. 4-65 - Concentrate most on movement from your shoulder.

Fig. 4-66 - Drawing a ripsaw back can create ruts that make it even harder to start the cut.

board, rather than the full flat edge. Use the back of the fingers of your other hand as a guide for the side of the sawplate to position the saw just where you want it. Start the cut using a forward stroke without any downward pressure. It may even help to think about lifting the saw off the work as you start. You can start by drawing the saw back if you prefer, but again you should think about almost lifting off the surface of the wood to avoid creating ruts. (Fig. 4-66) It often helps to start with shorter strokes as well, although the ultimate goal is long, smooth strokes that are closer to the full length of the saw. The short strokes are also easier to control as you work your way across the line on the top of the wood. Once you're all the way across the board you can concentrate on cutting down to the layout line on the front. Let the saw do the cutting. Don't be in a rush and apply too much pressure. If the overall motion is good and the saw is sharp, it should feel as if the weight of the saw is enough to cut. You may have to play around with downward pressure on the return stroke so that the saw doesn't bounce around or jump out of the cut. Differ-

Adjusting Drift

A saw that consistently drifts to one side may have a little extra set on the side it moves toward. Lightly dressing the set of the saw teeth with a sharpening stone can even out any irregularities and help the saw to cut more cleanly and accurately. Put a couple of strips of masking tape on the side of the saw plate that needs work – one just above the teeth and one about 1½" higher. The tape keeps you from scratching the saw plate. Lay the saw down on your workbench and take one or two very light passes along the length of the saw with a fine (#1,000 grit or thereabouts) stone.

ent saws will have slightly different needs for this.

Different strategies for cutting (starting with the saw flat across the top, starting on the far corner, etc.) are just strategies and are certainly worth experimenting with to see if they make things easier for you. They don't change the fundamentals, though.

Listen carefully to the sound of the saw. It should not sound choppy and rough, but rather smooth and flowing. Sawing should sound relaxed, not tense, and rhythmic rather than uneven. Sound is one of the most-ignored aspects of tool use, and it's amazing how much you can learn just by listening more. There is a surprisingly strong correlation between how the cut sounds and the overall cut quality.

Once you've got a smooth cutting motion, it can still take some experimentation to learn to cut straight down. One thing to check is if the workpiece is set up square in the vise. Your natural tendency should be to cut vertically; if the wood isn't vertical you're setting yourself up to cut at an angle. But it also takes time to get the feel of the saw. You may find that you need to learn what a vertical cut feels like. Does it need a little more lean to one side or the other? It's hard to tell this until you've gotten a feel for sawing, but an improperly set saw may tend to drift to one side. Make sure to keep all of the other fundamentals sound and stay relaxed as you experiment with this. Once you get a feel for cutting straight, you can start to work on cutting to a line.

Sandpaper

It may seem odd to consider sandpaper as a tool, but essentially, that is what it is. And because it's such a popular way to both remove and smooth wood (and wood finishes), it certainly merits some thought as to how it works, and how best to use it.

Sandpaper is easy to understand: The abrasives on the sandpaper scratch the wood easily. Make enough scratches and you wear through a layer of the wood. Make finer scratches with progressively finer grits and you'll remove the larger and coarser scratches, and eventually wind up with a smooth surface.

This smooth surface is very different from one that has been planed smooth. A sanded surface has been abraded smooth, and has countless tiny scratches. A planed surface has been sliced smooth. Setting aside arguments over the virtues of hand-tool work, a well-sanded surface will usually appear more even overall. It will also be slightly duller

Sandpaper

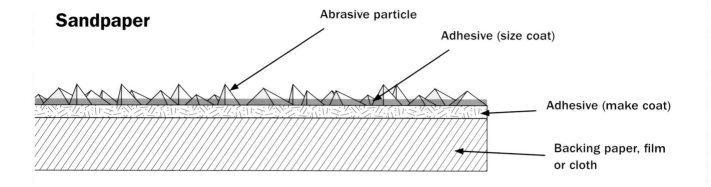

Abrasive particle

Adhesive (size coat)

Adhesive (make coat)

Backing paper, film or cloth

Fig. 4-67

because the scratches refract the light more than a cleanly sliced surface. A well-planed surface shows evidence of hand-work, revealing different passes with the plane as well as slight deterioration of the edge as the work progresses. The choice between the two is simply one of desired results; it's a question of style and design as much as one of quality.

There are certainly nuances to using sandpaper, and there's a big difference between sanding well and sanding poorly.

First, there are different types of sandpaper. Woodworkers aren't the only ones using this form of abrasive, and different types of sandpapers (and sanding films) are designed for different materials and/or finishes. They vary in the type of abrasive particles, the backing and the way the particles are bonded to the backing. (Fig. 4-67) Some sandpaper has added minerals (stearates) that can help prevent clogging up of the abrasive with sawdust and/or finish materials. Most useful for woodworking are garnet, aluminum oxide, silicon carbide (usually used with a lubricant, and generally only in finer grits, because this mineral is so sharp that coarser grits will leave deep scratches in the wood that are harder to get out), and stearated aluminum oxide, which has a soapy mineral coating added to prevent the paper from loading up with sawdust. The stearated papers are especially important when sanding finishes, which tend to clog up the paper more. Finer grits used on raw wood also benefit from the stearates, which will allow you to sand for longer without clogging.

There are also numerous systems for grading the coarseness of the grit. The three main systems are CAMI (the standard in the U.S., which uses numbers such as 120, 150, 220 and 320), FEPA (the European standard, designated with a "P" followed by a number, such as P220 and P280), and micron grading (based simply on the micron size of the particles, such as 15 micron or .5 micron).

The first and most important rule of sanding is that you

Grit Comparison

The American and European standards are complex formulas, and yield only average sizes of particles. Almost every source I checked had different micron equivalents. This chart is my attempt at a consensus. And relative gradations, not exact sizes, are what matter in woodworking.

CAMI (USA)	FEPA (Europe)	Micron Grade
	P80	197
80		192
	P100	156
100		141
	P120	127
120		116
	P150	97
150		93
180	P180	78
220		66
	P220	65
	P320	46
320		36
	P400	35
	P600	26
400		23

Fig. 4-68 - Sanding across the grain is a major taboo.

never sand across the grain. As with most good rules, there are a couple of exceptions, but these only apply when later sanding with the grain will eliminate the cross-grain scratches. These scratches are the reason you never want to go across the grain. Scratches across the grain actually cut the fibers in a way that is very obvious, especially on a finished piece. (Fig. 4-68) The scratches that go along the grain are generally indistinguishable from the grain itself. You don't have to worry much about grain direction on end grain though.

End grain poses its own problems. It takes a lot more work to sand than long grain, mostly because you're sanding the equivalent of the end of a bundle of tubes. They don't scratch away quite as easily, and you'll spend more time on cleaning up end-grain than you will on an equivalent amount of long grain. It's also a good idea to sand end grain to one finer grit level than the rest of the piece. This helps prevent the end grain from looking significantly darker than the rest of the wood once you apply the finish.

Sandpaper can be used by itself, or in conjunction with jigs (sanding pads or blocks). Sanding with just the sandpaper gives you a very direct feel for how the paper is cutting, and can actually be more aggressive than sanding with a block, which will distribute pressure over a wider area. However, sanding with just the sandpaper is more prone to uneven sanding, and sanding deeper into early wood, which can be softer than the late wood in some species. A block completely eliminates these problems.

The best way to sand by hand (without a sanding block) is to make a folded up "pad" of sandpaper. This gives you a better grip on the paper and distributes the pressure just a little. It's best if grit doesn't come into contact with other grit, which leaves a few ways to fold the paper. Smaller pieces can be folded in half. Larger pieces are best folded into thirds, like you would fold up a business letter. And a full sheet can be folded in quarters without grit contacting grit if you make a slit from the center of the paper along one of the creases. (Fig. 4-69)

The best sanding blocks have a little bit of give to the surface, which helps distribute the pressure. A block of wood with cork or hard felt on the bottom works very well. Curved sanding blocks (try a section of the offcut from sawing a curved part to shape) can work wonders on curved parts that can pose a real challenge to plane without running into grain direction issues.

This is sandpaper, after all, so it may seem silly to talk about how you hold it, or how you use it. Although you might never see a project and comment on – or even notice – how beautifully sanded it was, a poor sanding job could easily ruin an otherwise excellent project. With this inherent unfairness in mind, it does pay to work though some of the body mechanics involved.

There is a natural tendency to sand in arcs due to rotation about the elbow and/or shoulder. (Fig. 4-70) Work that will be stained or finished to a relatively glossy finish will tend to highlight these arcs, which do cut a bit across the grain. So it makes more sense to sand in a straight line out from and back toward your body. One problem

Fig. 4-69 - Sandpaper origami?

Fig. 4-70 - This is the natural tendency when sanding across the body. You can learn to overcome this.

with this is when you're sanding with just your hand; your fingers will push down more on the sandpaper than the spaces between your fingers (this will only be apparent with critical finish sanding).

You'll also run into trouble sanding large tabletops, where you may have to sand from side to side because you won't be able to reach far enough to sand the full length of the table. Learning to sand this way is actually a valuable skill, despite needing to compensate for the less-than-ideal body mechanics. The advantage here is that you don't have to worry about pushing a tool; there's not much application of force. So you can concentrate on just moving

the sandpaper in a straight line. Once you've done this for a while, you'll get the hang of it and the motion won't seem awkward.

Avoid sanding along edges with the raw edge of a piece of sandpaper (this applies to either a sanding bock or loose sandpaper). The raw edge can pick up any loose fibers and split them off of the wood. (This is analgous to a paper cut.) You should also pay careful attention not to round over the ends of boards as you sand. Instead, keep pressure firmly on the top surface. You can avoid rounding over edges by choosing narrow sanding blocks and concentrating on keeping pressure on the middle of the block.

Woodworking Machines

Woodworking machines can occasionally be a more forgiving when it comes to working with wood. This means that some of the time, you might actually get away with acting indifferently to wood's specific properties. But most often, you'll find wood to be remarkably just; if you break the rules, you'll pay the price. The fact that you're cutting faster with a powered machine doesn't change the way wood behaves. The tool interacts with the wood in the same way that hand tools do, based on the cutting action of the tool and the wood's grain. And a better understanding of exactly how the tool cuts and of the nature of wood will always lead to better results.

Table Saw

The exact origin of the circular saw is not clear. There is some thought that the earliest circular saws may have been used in Holland in the 16th or 17th century, but there is no concrete evidence. The first patent to include a circular saw was issued to Samuel Miller, of Southampton, England, and dates from 1777. And Tabitha Babbitt (who lived in the Shaker community in Harvard, Mass.) is also credited with the invention in 1813. Whatever the origin, the idea was both brilliant and simple. The rotating blade presents an endless procession of saw teeth, with no need for the wasted effort of the return stroke. The cutting action is very much the same as with a handsaw, and the teeth tend to be configured in similar ways. Basically, there are rip teeth, which are "filed" straight across, and crosscut teeth that have alternating points to score the fibers. There are also scores of refinements, but these are the fundamental variations.

The change from straight-line cutting to rotary cutting may not change the basics of each tooth's cut, but that spinning blade makes an enormous difference overall. There are significant benefits to this: mostly the speed of the cut; and the ability to feed the board past the blade in many different ways. But there are significant problems as well, mostly related to safety. That spinning blade will not only cut anything it encounters, but the rotational forces add significant risks.

What does it mean to have a blade powered by a one to 5-horsepower motor spinning at you at 3,000 to 4,000 revolutions per minute? It means there's a lot of potential to throw something in your direction at more than 100 mph. And you are responsible for the bulk of the control over the workpiece as it goes through the saw. Certainly the rip fence, the miter guide, or other accessories you might

Fig. 4-71 - The cut is more forward and down when the blade is lowered to a safer height.

Fig. 4-72 - With the blade raised up high, the saw cuts close to straight down.

add or make, are there to help control the workpiece. But there's no getting away from the fact that you have the prime responsibility for control, and anything that goes wrong with your control can cause serious problems.

Each tooth on the saw blade moves in an arc, emerging from the table at the back of the blade and moving forward and up to its maximum height, and then continues forward and back down under the table. The cut is supposed to take place only at the front of the arc. Exactly what that cut looks like depends on the height of the blade. With the blade projecting just above the wood, the general direction of the cutting arc is toward you and down; with the blade high up, more of the energy is directed down. (Figs. 4-71 & 4-72) Notice that this actually changes the type of cut from predominantly along the grain to mostly across the end grain. The former requires a little less force (although this is not generally a factor with a table saw). The latter is actually closer to how you rip by hand with a saw, but the added blade height is much more dangerous.

The front part of the blade should be the only part of the blade that contacts and cuts the wood. The teeth are wider than the rest of the saw plate, (either from set, as on a handsaw, or because the carbide teeth are wider than the steel plate) so the board shouldn't be in contact with that, and if everything lines up right, the back half of the blade (coming up and forward) should just slip through the already-cut kerf. But in reality, once the cut begins, any part of the blade that is above the table can wind up in contact with the wood. There are at least three things that can easily cause problems: the precision of the tool itself, the wood and – most significantly – the human input.

When the back of the blade comes in contact with the wood, it can cause all kinds of problems, from inaccurate, poor-quality cuts to catastrophic kick-backs.

If either the saw fence or saw table are not aligned with the saw blade, the wood can be forced into the back of the blade during a rip or crosscut with the miter guide. (Figs. 4-73 & 4-74)

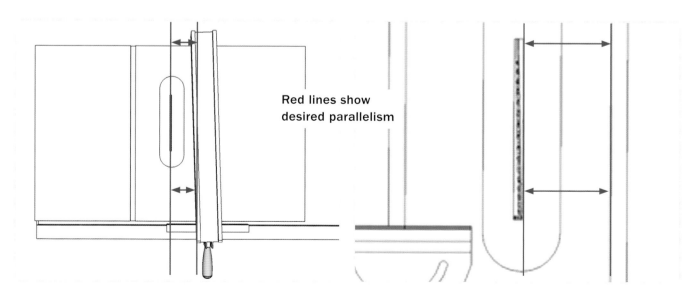

Red lines show desired parallelism

Fig. 4-73 - If the rip fence isn't parallel to the blade (or angled slightly away from the blade), boards will be forced into the back of the blade when ripping.

Fig. 4-74 - If the saw table isn't parallel to the blade, the miter slots won't be parallel either. This can push a board into the rising teeth at the back of the blade when crosscutting.

Table Saw Safety

The table saw is a dangerous tool that requires nothing less than your full attention. Learn as much as you can about the tool, and never get so comfortable or complacent that you fail to pay attention to the safety rules.

- Always wear eye protection. Always. And ear and lung protection too.
- Never wear loose clothing or accessories that could possibly get caught in any machine. Long hair can also get caught in the machine, and should be secured so that it will not come loose.
- Always maintain your balance and good footing.
- Never work distracted – you have to focus 100 percent on what you're doing at all times on the table saw. Avoid responding to distractions until you have finished your cut and the saw has stopped moving.
- Either use the guards that came with the saw, or replace them with better guards that you will use almost all of the time.
- Always use the saw with a splitter or riving knife. If it gets in the way of a specific cut and you remove it, be sure to replace it immediately after the cut. Or find a better and safer way to make the cut.
- The wood must be under your control at all times. The natural tendency of the saw is to throw something back at you, and you are responsible for all of the control that keeps that from happening. You need the assistance of – at the very least – the rip fence, the miter guide or other jigs. You also need the work to be firmly on the saw table. You may also find featherboards, anti-kickback devices and other accessories helpful in keeping the work under control. Never cut freehand.
- The main elements of control at the table saw are as follows:
1. The work must always be securely down on the table.
2. Rip cuts must always stay tight to the rip fence.
3. Hold the work securely to the miter guide or crosscut sled when these are in use. Don't push on the offcut section when using the miter guide.
- The table saw is not the right tool for small parts – anything smaller than a foot in length should be cut somewhere else (unless it is held in a larger jig designed to hold small parts securely).
- Never leave anything loose or unsupported between the rip fence and the blade. This is a major invitation for kick-back. Never set up a cut that will leave the offcut there.
- Never use miter guide and rip fence together (this will leave a cut-off between the rip fence and the blade).
- Always push a board completely past the blade when cutting (so it doesn't remain between the blade and the fence).
- Don't cut narrow strips between the rip fence and blade (flex can lead to jamming and kickback). In-

The wood can also distort in a variety of ways during the cut; either closing up on the blade or changing shape in a way that makes it difficult (or impossible) to keep it against the rip fence or on the table. The splitter (or riving knife) – now required on all new saws but worth retrofitting to any saw – is a primary defense against these problems. (Fig. 4-75) The splitter is also supposed to prevent the wood from clamping down on or jamming into the back of the blade, but it is not always successful at that. It acts as a guard for the back part of the blade that can cause so much trouble. Even so, under the wrong circumstances, the saw blade can, rather than cut the wood, grab it and throw it off the saw at great speed, and with potentially catastrophic results.

Anything jammed between the rip fence (or any other stationary object on the saw table) and the spinning blade can be sent back out of the saw at tremendous speed – in excess of 100 mph. And if you fail to keep a board tightly against the fence or securely on the saw table, you can also run into trouble. You lose contact with one of the primary

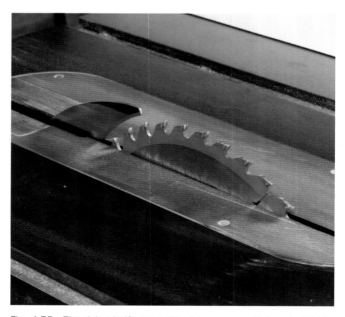

Fig. 4-75 - The riving knife (or splitter) is an essential part of table saw safety.

stead, set up the cut so that the narrow strips fall away freely on the left side of the blade (assuming the fence is to the right). You'll have to re-set the fence for each cut.

- Never bring your hand close to a spinning blade under any circumstances. Shut the saw down before retrieving offcuts or cleaning away debris.
- Always work deliberately and carefully.
- Keep your hands away from the blade! Keep proper push sticks handy and use them when necessary. The best push sticks allow you to push forward and keep the work securely on the table. But your hands are better at this. If your hands do not need to get close to the blade, use them; you'll have more control with your hands.
- Keep your hands out of the path of the blade, both

The push stick style at the front should be avoided. It helps you push, but it doesn't really help hold the work flat on the table, which is an essential part of control at the saw. The two other push sticks help push just as well, but offer far more overall control and hold the work securely on the table.

front and back. Never reach around behind the saw to pull a board through or to grab a part; a kickback could pull or push your hand over the blade.

- Although a board that kicks back can bounce off things and go anywhere, the most likely path is directly in line with the blade. Don't work while anyone else is in this kickback path. Stay out of this path except at the very end of a cut, when you step forward to push the work beyond the blade.
- Body and hand positions are crucial on the table saw, and not just for getting the best results. Here, these are also safety issues. Your body and hands need to be in the right place at all times. (See the body position section below). Leave a margin for error.
- If there's any question in your mind about the safety of a cut, find a different tool to do the job.

Never try to get away with something on the table saw. It may be possible to do something stupid now and then, but without an adequate margin for error, when things go wrong you will pay for it. Listen to the voice in your head that says something is wrong or dangerous before you do it, and find another way. There's always another way to do something. If it seems like a waste of time to figure out a safer way, weigh the cost of an injury in both time and money into your calculations. Most accidents happen either after proceeding with something that you know is a bad idea, or when you are tired or impaired.

means of controlling the board.

This all leads to a random feeling about safety at the table saw as well, a sense that anything could happen at any time. That's not just the saw; the wood, and its tendency to distort as you cut it, contributes to the unpredictability. Unfortunately, there's also a feeling that you might be able to get away with something some of the time. The goal then has to be to increase your margin of safety, and never get into a situation where if something out of the ordinary were to happen, it would cause an accident.

You can operate a saw safely, but it requires constant effort in many areas. You need to learn as much about saw safety as possible, learn the right ways of working, have the right guards and safety equipment (and use them) and never slack off in your efforts to stay safe.

Proper Body and Hand Position

Good body position is important with hand tools because it's hard to get accurate results and the proper force otherwise. With machines, good body position and use

Fig. 4-76 - Hiding behind the fence is no way to cut. There's no good way to hold the work securely against the fence.

Fig. 4-78 - This stance should be familiar to you by now.

are important not just for accurate results, but for overall safety as well. Proper body position is not always obvious on the table saw. Many woodworkers fear this machine, and feel safer if they "hide" behind the rip fence. (Fig. 4-76) Unfortunately, this position is actually dangerous. It significantly reduces control over the workpiece, and creates a much greater safety hazard.

Ripping

Stand at your saw facing the rip fence with your hips at about a 45° angle (most fences are to the right of the blade, in which case you would stand to the left of the blade facing the fence). Notice that this keeps you out of the direct path of the blade. It also puts you in a position of great control; you can easily push the board tight to the fence, which is the most important way to keep control over the cut. Your feet

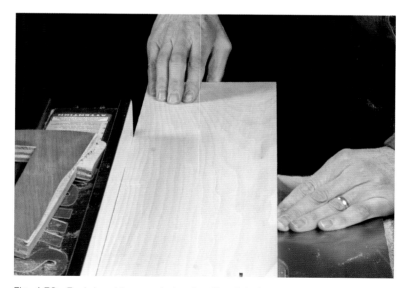

Fig. 4-79 - Each hand has a role to play. The right hand is pushing and keeping the board level; the left holds it against the rip fence and down on the table if necessary.

The Thumb Trick

Switching from feeding a board with four fingers underneath the board to feeding with your thumb and the rest of the fingers on top of the board – without stopping to change hand position – is a little bit of thumb magic.

 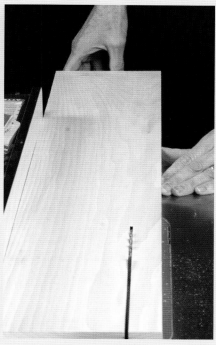 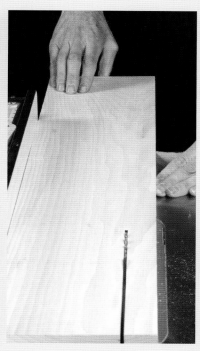

The "thumb trick" starts with your hand palm up and pushing the board forward.

Roll your wrist in, and place the side of your thumb against the end of the board. This happens while you continue to push the board forward.

Finally, bring your four fingers on top of the board, while the thumb continues to push forward.

should be in the basic woodworking stance: front foot forward; rear foot back and angled; knees slightly bent and hips forward. (Fig. 4-78) The size of the board may determine exactly where you stand; you'll be farther back with a longer board so you can balance and feed it properly. As you get closer to the saw you may want to brace your body against the machine. Having your body close will give you more stability and control, and does not necessarily mean your hands will be any closer to the blade.

Your hands each have a different role. The hand closer to the fence (the right hand, if the fence is to your right) is the feed hand; it pushes the board forward. (Fig. 4-79) Keep this hand level as it moves forward or you'll wind up lifting the board off the blade. This will happen either if your hand is too high and directly lifts the work off the table, or, more likely, too low, where you'll lever it off the table. You'll usually start with this hand at the end of the board. The forearm of your pushing hand should be roughly aligned with the direction of cut. This is not as critical as with hand tools, and you shouldn't worry about perfect alignment.

The opposite hand should be planted on the saw table a few inches ahead of the blade guard. This hand is responsible for holding the work against the rip fence, and also down on the table. You may want to let the wood slide past your fingers as they press against the board, or walk your fingers along the edge of the board as you press against the fence, but this hand really shouldn't move. In either case, it can take some practice to coordinate the movements of your two hands.

What do you watch when ripping? There are two things. You should focus on keeping the edge of the board tight to the rip fence, but you also need to be sure your hands are always well away from the blade. You don't have to watch the cut, other than to be aware of the blade enough to keep your hands a few inches (at least) away.

The forearm on your pushing arm should generally be aligned with the direction of the push. With longer boards you can start with your hand in back of you (palm facing up). But at some point, you'll have to switch your hand position to one that will work on the saw table; the palm-up position won't work well. To avoid stopping and re-positioning your hand, there's a cool little maneuver that you can do with your thumb.

Cutting long boards often means that you'll have to start with your body farther away from the saw, then move forward as the cut progresses. But you still need to hold the work tight to the fence and flat on the table. The balance and pressure required to do this leads to an unusual walk. This is the most controlled way to move forward. Start out in the basic, balanced position. Keep your knees bent, with hips forward and level as you move your rear foot, still pointing off to the side, to the front. Then bring the other foot forward, and keep it pointing forward. With your feet pointed in different directions as you walk you have more control over your body, and therefore over the board that you're moving. Keeping your knees bent and hips level as you do this walk will also help keep the board flat on the table. (Figs. 4-80, 4-81 & 4-82)

With any of the rip cuts, you will have to step forward at the very end with your back foot so you can push the board all the way past the blade. This does mean stepping into the path of the blade for a moment, but getting the board all the way through the cut is vital, and with most of the board already through the blade, there is less risk of kickback.

Once your pushing hand is alongside the fence, you should also hook some of your fingers over the fence; this guards against accidentally letting this hand wander away from the fence as you pass by the blade. If your hand will be anywhere within a few inches from the blade, you should switch to a push stick instead. Always keep a push stick handy on the saw for rip cuts. (Fig. 4-83)

It's a good idea to practice moving boards over the saw with the machine turned off and the blade below the table.

Crosscutting

Cross cutting is generally much easier than ripping. The main concern is keeping the work

Fig. 4-80 - The long board dance.

Fig. 4-81 - The rear foot steps forward, but still points off to the side. This looks more awkward than it is.

Fig. 4-82 - And finally, step back into the basic woodworking stance to complete the cut.

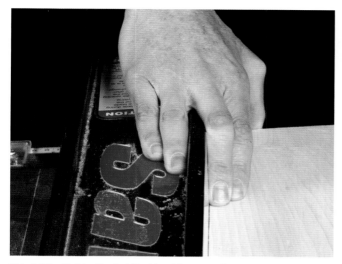

Fig. 4-83 - Get in the habit of hooking your fingers onto the fence when you're pushing through on a rip cut.

Fig. 4-84 - Upright work is easy with a good jig.

securely against the miter guide. If a board is either too wide (and the miter guide doesn't start out on the saw table), or too long for easy control with the miter guide, you should switch instead to a crosscut sled, an important table saw accessory that should be standard in every shop. You might also choose a different tool altogether.

The basic woodworking position is used here as well, with the body in close to (and possibly braced against) the saw. Hold the work against the miter guide with two hands, and leave the offcut alone until you shut down the saw. If you need to support a longer offcut, it's a good idea to clamp or screw a wooden extension to the miter guide that will push it past the blade. Pushing with your hand you risk pinching it against the blade. Make sure the rip fence is well out of the way for all crosscutting.

It's a good idea to use a backing board (sometimes

called a sacrificial fence) with either the miter guide or a crosscut sled to avoid splintering the near edge of the board, where the saw exits the cut. Remember: Never use the rip fence along with the other guide.

Upright Work

Ripping and crosscutting are the best-known ways to work on a table saw but they're not the only ways. You can also do upright work. And this is where you can do some of the most interesting and creative stuff. Upright work is always done with the assistance of jigs of various kinds: some that ride in the miter slot or slots (commercial tenoning jigs, for example); others that straddle the rip fence. The workpiece should be clamped to whatever jig you use. Body position is generally the same as for crosscuts. (Fig. 4-84 & 4-85)

A Shop-made Upright Table Saw Jig

Build the jig to fit your rip fence.

The jig slides on the saw's rip fence.

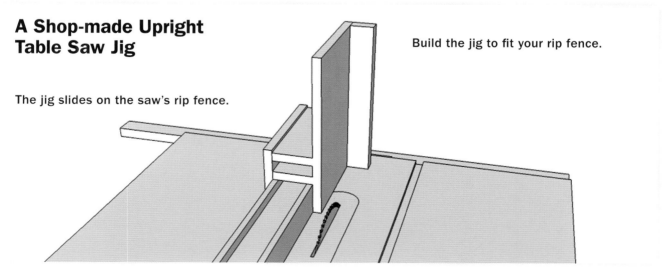

Fig. 4-85

Cut Quality

The ideal table saw cut leaves a straight, smooth edge that requires a minimal amount of clean up afterward. In order to get a cut like this, you need to feed the wood evenly, and minimize starting and stopping. You need to keep the board securely against the fence and on the table the entire time. While it's certainly possible to stop and re-start a rip cut, this usually leads to an indentation and possibly a burn mark on the edge. The best cuts are made with a continuous and even feed. But on a long and awkward board, you're better off stopping and repositioning your hands than struggling and getting your guide hand into a more dangerous position. A featherboard can help secure the board to the fence and can minimize indented cuts and burning even if you have to stop.

Learning how to feed smoothly takes experimentation and practice, just as learning to feed safely does. Different boards will require different strategies. You can experiment as much as you want in complete safety with the saw off and the blade lowered beneath the surface of the table.

Cutting speed – how fast you push the wood into the saw – is also important. You need to go slowly enough to

Fig. 4-86 - Too fast. Too slow. And just right. The "Goldilocks and the Three Bears" of woodworking.

give the saw a chance to actually cut what is being pushed at it, but quickly enough that the saw doesn't burn the wood from excess friction. You may have to experiment a little here as well to get the feel for different boards and thicknesses. Over time, you'll learn to automatically adjust the feed based on the feel of the cut. (Fig. 4-86)

The Jointer

The jointer functions very much like a motorized handplane. In fact, you can use a handplane clamped upside down in a vise as a form of small jointer. Thinking about the jointer as simply a motorized version of a plane can help you learn to use the tool better as well. The jointer is not an automatic tool. You need to think about how you're going to use it, and you have to pay attention to the wood in many of the same ways you would if you were working with hand tools.

Of course, the actual workings of the jointer are more complex than those of a handplane. The jointer has a rotating cutterhead in place of the fixed blade of the handplane. The cutterhead has knives (or carbide inserts) set at a fairly steep cutting angle:

How the Jointer Works

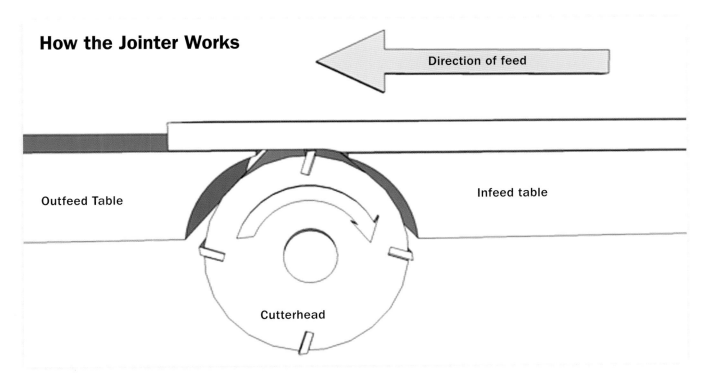

Direction of feed

Outfeed Table

Infeed table

Cutterhead

Fig. 4-87

the equivalent of a 60° to 80° plane iron. As the wood passes over the cutter-head, each knife or cutter takes a small curved chip out of the board. The steep angle of the knives means the cut is somewhat less likely to tear out beyond the intended cut, but this in no way eliminates this tendency. The cuts also leave a slightly scalloped surface, not a truly flat one. Whether this is glaringly obvious or almost too subtle to see depends on the cutting geometry of the knives the speed of the cutterhead, the sharpness of the knives and the speed at which the wood passes over the cutterhead.

The cutterhead is located between the infeed table and the outfeed table. (Fig. 4-87) The height of the infeed table relative to the highest point of the knives as they rotate determines the depth of the cut that the jointer will take. The outfeed table is set to exactly the same height as the knives at the top of their cut, so when the wood comes off the cutterhead, it slides directly onto the outfeed table. This is the way the jointer flattens a board; the just-cut surface registers on the out-feed table and the rest of the board gets cut in that same geometric plane. Keeping the board flat on the outfeed table is much more important than keeping it flat on the infeed table.

Using the Jointer

The jointer is not an easy machine to master, even though it looks like you simply pass the board over the surface. There are a lot of things to contend with as you work, especially as you deal with bigger boards. Your main goal

when using the jointer is obviously to either straighten an edge or to flatten the face of a board. But to get to that result, you need to be able to feed the board through with steady pressure on the outfeed table and, in the case of edge jointing, against the fence as well. You need to be able to "read" a board to get the necessary information both on grain direction (to minimize tear-out) and how the board is out of flat or true. Boards of different sizes pose different challenges as well. And of course, you need to understand how you can best use your body to get the board over the machine effectively.

Check the wood to see what you need to do before you begin. Does the grain emerge in one particular direction? The board should be oriented with the grain emerging toward the rear of the board (on the bottom). If you can't

Dealing with Twist

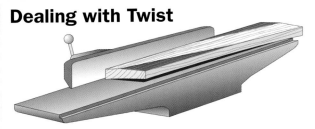

After running one face over the jointer, the board is flipped over to show half of the twist is removed from each end of the board (in red), leaving a more useable board than if all the twist were removed from one end.

Fig. 4-88

Jointer Safety

The jointer is a dangerous machine. Keeping your hands well away from the cutterhead is critically important. That means being very careful with the sizes of pieces you edge or surface joint. The jointer is not the right machine for dealing with small pieces. No board shorter than 12" should be jointed. Boards narrower than 3" are too dangerous to edge-joint without appropriate push blocks or featherboards. Boards thinner than ½" are dangerous to face joint, and risk shattering in addition to the danger to your hands.

- Never use the jointer without the appropriate guards in place. But be aware that the guards do not necessarily protect you in all situations, and you should act as cautiously as you would if the guards were not in place.
- Use push blocks to keep your hands out of the way, especially with smaller boards.
- Wear the usual eye, ear and lung protection.
- Be sure that you do not have any loose clothing, accessories or hair that might get caught in the machine.
- Never push a board through with your thumb or other fingers on the back edge of the board when surface jointing. Use heavy-duty push blocks when necessary.
- In general, the jointer shouldn't be used for aggressive cuts. Consider $\frac{1}{16}$" depth a maximum for clear boards, less for difficult or knotty wood. The deeper the cut, the greater the force pushing back at you, and consequently, the harder you'll have to push. This will give you less control. There is also a greater risk of the board kicking back, and a greater risk of serious tear-out in the wood if you push too hard.
- Pushing the work through on the outfeed table is ideal – because your hands are beyond the cutterhead at all times, and you're not at all likely to slip into the cutter. But it doesn't work for all boards.
- Keep your hands from places where they might slip into the cutterhead. The outfeed table is safest (you'll slip away from the cutter). Brace yourself against the machine so you're well balanced when reaching forward to the outfeed side.
- Experiment and practice with the machine off. Maintaining balance and control is essential. This experimentation will allow you to develop strategies even for awkward boards. And practice will leave you more comfortably in control.

Every board poses its own challenges. Hand positions will be different for face jointing and edge jointing, and for tall pieces and shorter ones. Long pieces pose different challenges than shorter ones. Practice how you will feed boards through the machine with the machine off. Watch your hand positions for potential problems. Set up infeed and outfeed supports at the right heights as needed. If you use an assistant, make sure he or she knows the role, and won't pull you off balance and into the cutter. Practice together if necessary.

American and European-style jointers have different safety guards, and the guards actually have an impact on how you should use the tool. American guards usually look like a pork chop, and pivot out of the way to allow the board to pass through (below).

European guards don't move during use, but have adjustable support arms that allow you to adjust both their height and distance from the jointer fence (below). The guards each have their plusses and minuses, but both work well.

The European-style guard should be set just high enough to allow the board to pass beneath it. It will then remain in place over the cutterhead throughout the cut. An American-style guard is better suited for use with push blocks, because the guard will swing out of the way, allowing you to use the blocks continuously. This allows you to keep even pressure on the board throughout the cut.

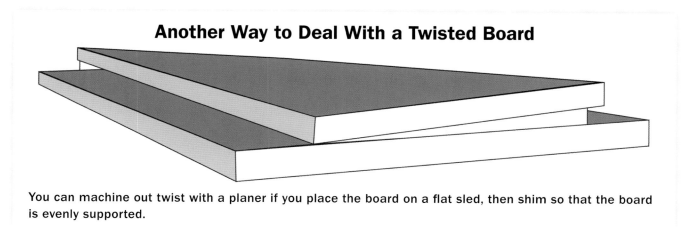

Another Way to Deal With a Twisted Board

You can machine out twist with a planer if you place the board on a flat sled, then shim so that the board is evenly supported.

Fig. 4-89

figure out the grain, you may just have to make a cut, then examine the results. If you see significant tear-out, try jointing from the other direction. Is the wood cupped, bowed or twisted? With a cupped or bowed board, you should put the concave side down. If the board is both cupped and bowed, but in different directions, the bow should take precedence and go concave side down.

Twist presents a different challenge. If you hold the board so that the front end of the twisted board is flat on the infeed table, you may wind up cutting all of the twist off only one corner at back of the board. That corner can wind up thinned down to almost nothing. (Fig. 4-88) You should try to start the board so that you joint out just half of the twist on the front of the board, and half on the back. You can accomplish this by controlling where you put pressure with your hands as you start the cut. Once you've made your first pass, there should be enough to register the remaining cuts at the proper angle. If you're not comfortable with this, you may need to switch to a different tool to remove the twist. Flattening can be done selectively with handplanes, or even with a planer, using a sled on which you carefully shim the board so the machine removes the wood evenly from the twist face. (Fig. 4-89)

Face Jointing

Face jointing is simpler than edge jointing, because you need only worry about keeping the board on the table. It's a little harder (physically), though, because so much more of the cutter is engaged in the wood. Keeping the wood down on the table and moving smoothly and continu-

Fig. 4-90 - Good position at the jointer is in close, braced against the machine and leaning in a bit. Your right hand is well positioned to push. You'll have to make do with the slightly off-axis push from the left hand.

Fig. 4-91 - In the starting position at the jointer, there's more pressure down with the left hand at the start of the cut.

ously through the machine requires keeping your body in the best position possible. You'll have to learn to cope with the misaligned position of your left hand and arm when you try to push forward in a continuous feed. You'll find that it's harder to push forward with your arm angled across your body this way. Unfortunately, there isn't a better position to work with. (Fig. 4-90)

Position yourself in the basic woodworking stance at the side of the machine along the infeed table. Brace yourself against the machine so you can lean your body a little over the work. This will help you to push the board with more control. As is true with the table saw, this leaning into the

machine may feel more dangerous. But it puts you in a much better position to control what is happening.

The seemingly safer position farther away from the tool can lead to loss of control over the workpiece, and as a result, is more dangerous. There's more control in close to your body.

Start with your left hand on top of the board at the front. (Fig. 4-91) Use a push block if you have an American-style guard. This hand will be responsible initially for keeping the board securely on the table as you start the cut. Your right hand is the main pushing hand, and can be either at the back of the board or somewhere in the mid-

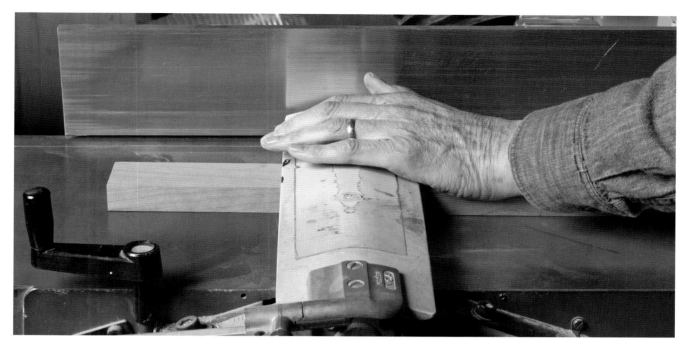

Fig. 4-92 - Begin to bridge over the European-style guard using the heel of your hand to maintain downward pressure.

Fig. 4-93 - Lower the fingers and lift the heel of your hand as you move forward over the guard.

dle, depending on the board's length. You should not hook your fingers over the back end of the board. Instead, use the heel of your palm or a push block.

You should try to keep your forearm mostly aligned with the direction of the cut. You won't have the same kind of alignment you see with a handplane or chisel. Instead, your lower arm will angle up. This is in keeping with a push that is both down and forward.

As soon as the cut starts, your left hand will move forward onto the outfeed table. This is easy and obvious with the American-style guard and a push block in hand, but it requires a little bridging maneuver with a European-style guard. As the board moves forward your hand will approach the guard. Raise your fingers, while keeping pressure on the board with the heel of your hand. (Fig. 4-92) As you continue to push the board forward, your fingers

Fig. 4-94 - At the other side of the bridge, your entire hand should once again maintain downward pressure.

will pass over the guard. As soon as they've reached the other side, your should put them back on the board, fingertips first. (Fig. 4-93) Then transfer the pressure to the fingertips as you raise up the heel of your hand so it can pass over the guard. Finally, put the heel of your hand back down on the board to continue the pressure. (Fig. 4-94)

As soon as you can, you should switch your right hand to the outfeed table along with your left.(Fig. 4-95) Then you can do a hand-over-hand push for the rest of the board. Even pressure on the outfeed table is the best way to ensure a flat cut on the jointer. It's also much safer to

have your hands beyond the cutterhead. Just make sure the rest of your body is well positioned to push and maintain even pressure on the outfeed table.

Face jointing (and thickness planing as well) usually comes before edge jointing. It is harder to put a straight edge on a board that isn't flat on at least one face.

Edge Jointing

The challenge of edge jointing is to keep the face of the board tight to the fence as you pass it over the jointer. Your left hand is responsible for keeping the board against

Fig. 4-95 - Two hands on the outfeed table is safer.

Fig. 4-96 - Edge jointing is similar, but you have to keep the work tight to the fence as well. Pressure with the left hand should be mostly toward the fence.

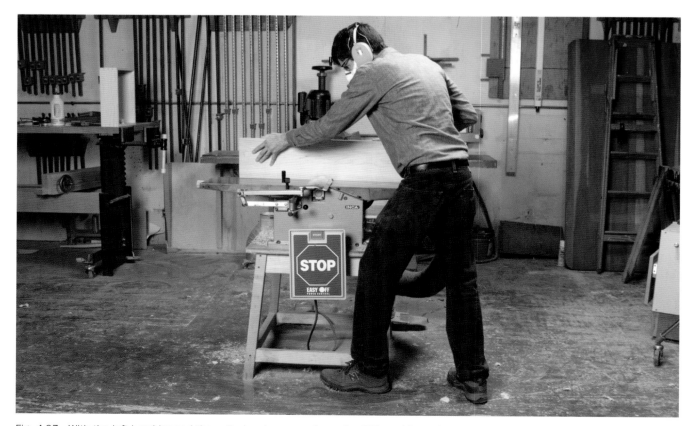

Fig. 4-97 - With the left hand beyond the cutterhead, you can lower it a little and keep the pressure against the fence.

Fig. 4-98 - Finish up the edge with both hands on the outfeed table side maintaining pressure against the fence.

the fence. At the beginning of the cut, it has the second-ary responsibility of pressing down (hook your thumb over the top of the board while you press the board against the fence with your other fingers). You should move this hand to the outfeed table as soon as possible. Once the board is far enough along that you don't have to worry about hold-ing it down on the outfeed table, plant you hand on the table while you push the board in against the fence. The right hand is the pushing hand, and once again, the fore-arm should be roughly aligned with the cut. A push stick similar to one used on the table saw should be used with narrower boards to keep your hand out of harm's way. Boards that are wider than the fence give you the oppor-tunity to switch both hands to the out-feed table and push the board hand-over-hand. (Figs. 4-96, 4-97 & 4-98)

Cut Quality

Cut quality on the jointer comes down to a few basic fac-tors. You need to keep the board on the table, and feed it over the jointer at the proper speed. Push too quickly, and the jointer will cut a coarse, scalloped edge. Hesitate and stop, and you may leave burn marks or small ridges. This may be unavoidable with larger boards. And of course, you need to pay attention to grain direction to avoid (or at least minimize) tear-out.

Fig. 4-99 - Pushing straight down on this band saw blade (held here between blocks) deflects the blade off the one side.

The Band Saw

The band saw is a very versatile shop machine. It's purchase is often bypassed in the hurry to get a table saw, which is often considered the "core" of the shop. But the band saw is both safer and, in many ways, a more versatile machine than the table saw. Most people think of it strictly as a machine for cutting curves, at which it excels. But the band saw is a great tool for ripping wood, re-sawing (rip-

A Foot Rest

One of my band saws has an open stand, with a cross-rail about 7" up from the floor. More often than not, I find myself putting my front foot up on that rail. I find that, especially for detail work, I like to lean in over the saw. Elevating the front foot helps to ease the pressure on the lower back, and is much more comfortable when I'm doing a lot of work at the saw. This position doesn't work with larger pieces, but I don't need to lean in for these. For that, the basic woodworking stance is fine.

Step up to the task by putting your foot up (here, on one of the stretchers on the saw's base); it's a comfortable alternative to the basic stance.

ping a board on edge) to create thinner stock or veneer, and even cutting a wide array of joinery. The band saw requires skilled input, however, to get the best results. Even then, cuts made with this saw often require further refinement with jointing, planing or smoothing.

The band saw cutting action is very much like that of a handsaw. But the band saw does not have the deep blade of a handsaw, or a stiff back. Tension, and the guides that support the blade just above the cut and below the saw table, keep the band saw blade straight and on track. Band saws have a way to adjust this tension; this is typically a spring in conjunction with a lead screw. The amount of tension depends on the blade type and size, and should be set according to the saw and the blade manufacturer's recommendations. If there is not enough tension, the blade will deflect as the board is pushed against it. (Fig. 4-99) As the blade deflects, it will twist to one side or the other, and ultimately will cut a curved kerf. (Fig. 4-100) This is most common when re-sawing. Not only does this result in a cut that is different from what you're expecting (which can be dangerous because the blade will emerge somewhere you're not expecting it), there's also much more friction in the cut, and it will be much harder to push the wood through. This may even bind enough to bring the saw to a stop in the cut. A dull blade, which will require more pressure when feeding the wood, will often cause the same problem even under proper tension.

Using the Band Saw

The most important skill on the band saw is cutting accurately to a line. And this is the main reason that most people don't rely on this tool more. It takes a well-tuned

Fig. 4-100 - A curved cut can result from blade deflection.

machine, a good blade and a fair bit of practice to reliably cut where you want to cut. And you can't generally expect the cut to be as smooth as a table saw cut. But it can certainly be smooth enough.

Good body position will help you to feed the work through the machine with the least effort and the greatest control. The basic woodworking stance is once again the foundation. (Fig. 4-101)

Keep one hand firmly planted on the saw table, at least a couple of inches from the blade, to help guide the work. The other hand feeds. The feed hand is doing the critical work; your forearm should be aligned more or less in the direction of the cut for the greatest efficiency. This hand is also supporting the work so it stays flat on the table. The guide hand (on the table) helps with fine adjustments. Keeping your hands spread apart like this will give you more control.(Fig. 4-102)

You need to watch where you're cutting, and this takes both aligning your dominant eye with the path of the blade, and then relying on that eye for most of your guidance. But you need both eyes open so you can see more of the path to be cut. This is somewhat like driving a car; you don't just watch exactly where you're driving, you need to look ahead to where you need to drive. Unlike driving, though, on the band saw, where you need to cut is closer to you, not farther away. It takes practice to get used to steering the work from behind; it's not something that you can really expect to do naturally. Concentrate on feeding the wood smoothly through the saw in a broad, sweeping motion rather than making small and halting cuts. It may be best to practice feeding smoothly without trying to cut to a line first, much as you would do with a hand saw.

The Router

The router is one of the simplest of machines; at its most basic, it is just a way to hold a spinning cutter (router bit). The vast selection of router bits coupled with the variety of common router configurations (fixed base, plunge base,

Fig. 4-101 - Good body position at the band saw involves spreading your hands apart to give you better control.

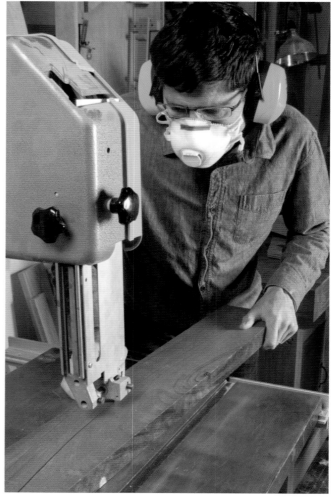

Fig. 4-102 - In another view of work at the band saw, my right hand is mostly hidden by the blade guard, but it's planted on the table, and helps to guide the cut.

Band Saw Safety

As on all power tools, you should always wear eye, ear and lung protection when using the band saw. Unlike the table saw, the direction of cut on the band saw is straight down toward the saw's table. This means that there is almost none of the unpredictability of the table saw, with its rotating blade. A workpiece left in mid-cut on the band saw table will not move; there is no risk of kick-back. There is also much less blade in the cut, which makes it highly unlikely that the blade will bind in the cut (unless the blade has deflected and curved). But the band saw is just like other power tools in that it doesn't know the difference between wood and flesh, and will cut either with equal ease and efficiency. So you need to keep your hands clear of the area around the blade and maintain your balance and control over the work. Minimize blade exposure and blade deflection by keeping the upper blade guide just above the work. Keep in mind that there is no guard to protect you from the blade before or after the cut has been made. You need to make sure your hands are well clear of the blade as it emerges at the end of the cut. If there's no room to keep your hands clear (as might be the case when re-sawing a thin board), you can pull the last bit of board through from the back of the saw. The other critical aspect to safely using a band saw is that the work must be firmly supported by the table at all times. This seems like an obvious statement, but it applies to some less-than-obvious cuts. Anything that doesn't make contact with the table directly underneath the blade poses a risk. This includes most cuts on round stock (either ripping or crosscutting), some cuts on curved pieces, and some angled cuts. In any of these, the blade can grab the work and throw it down on the table, or bind up the blade. This can add just the kind of random mayhem you need to avoid.

Use infeed or outfeed supports to help you keep larger boards level and securely on the table.

Keep your hands away from the blade at the end of the cut.

Clamp round stock securely before attempting to cut it. It wants to roll into the blade otherwise.

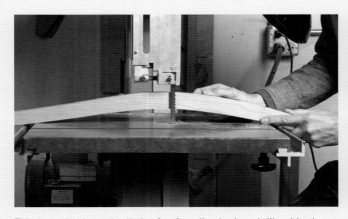

This is probably at the limit of safety. I've had work like this tip over and slam down to the table.

The work here is better supported on the band saw table.

or trim router) and methods of use (hand-held, in a router table, or in conjunction with a wide range of jigs) means it's hard to even think of the router as a single tool with a specific purpose. Indeed, there are few things that a router, in conjunction with some sort of jig, cannot tackle. Routers are good for cutting profiles on edges, mortise and tenon joinery, inlay work, dovetails, rabbets, duplicating parts and much more.

The cutting action for most router bits is very much like what takes place on a jointer; the rotating cutter enters the wood and essentially cuts out a small curved chip of wood. This leaves a very slightly scalloped surface, just as it does on the jointer. The rate of feed, cutting geometry, the grain direction in the wood, and the sharpness of the cutter will all have an impact on the final cut quality.

Spiral up-cut or down-cut bits (the side of an end-mill type bit is one example) cut along their sides with a shearing action, and can handle situations where the grain is difficult much better than can a straight bit. (Fig. 4-102)

Most of the time, you feed the work against the direction of the rotating bit, just as you feed the work against the oncoming rotation of the cutterhead on the jointer (or on the table saw, for that matter). Another more concrete way to look at this is that you move the router so that the work is to the left of the router bit when you're pushing the router away from yourself. (Fig. 4-103)

You'll see all of the expected results as the cutter interacts with the wood; grain direction matters. The spinning router bit can lift up wood fibers that may break off deeper than the intended cut. In addition, because the cutter is not always set to cut the full width of an edge, there is the risk of fibers breaking out above or below the cut. (Fig. 4-104) Cutting across end grain will likely blow out the fibers at the end of the board, as you would find with any cross-grain cut. Clamping a backing board in place at the end of the cut can prevent that blow-out.

Chamfering the back corner usually works as well.

Fig. 4-102 - A straight bit on the left and a spiral bit on the right.

The router seems like a very aggressive machine, but that's not an invitation to overwork the tool. As with any tool, the bigger the cut you take, the lower the quality of the cut. The router bit can only remove a certain amount of wood with each pass before it starts running into excessive resistance. Trying to take off more wood may cause compression of the wood, tearing of the fibers, and possibly a router-bit gullet clogged with chips. The bit will start to bounce off the wood a little, causing additional vibration. And this will affect both the quality of the cut and the size or location of the cut. It comes back to the same rule of using your body; working hard and accurate work don't go together. (Fig. 4-105)

For accurate work and smoother cuts, try to keep the router "quiet." That may sound ridiculous; the router is one of the noisiest machines in the shop. But it gets even louder when it's overworked. Try to regulate your cuts so it doesn't get any louder than it already is.

Because there are so many ways to use the router, it may seem like there should be more ways to use your body

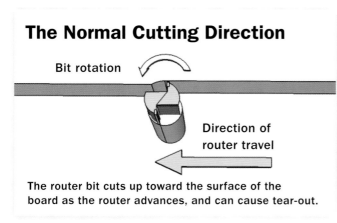

The Normal Cutting Direction

Bit rotation

Direction of router travel

The router bit cuts up toward the surface of the board as the router advances, and can cause tear-out.

Fig. 4-103

Fig. 4-104 - The router has a tendency to blow out wood below the surface of the cut.

Climb Cutting

Much of the time, you can eliminate the risk of fibers breaking out above or below the cut by taking a light "climb cut" before you make a full-depth cut in the usual direction.

When you're cutting normally with a router, you move the router bit into the edge of a board against the direction of rotation. As you move the router forward, the bit exits the wood in a previously uncut area. This can lift up the unsupported wood fibers and cause tear-out. (See Fig. 4-104 opposite page.) A climb cut is made in the opposite direction from a typical router cut, and in the same direction as the cutter rotation. When climb cutting, as you move the router forward, the bit rotates and enters into the uncut wood. Because it is cutting down into the wood, there is no tendency to tear-out.

Why not climb cut all of the time? The main reason is that it is dangerous. The router bit wants to pull the router along the work and this can lead to a loss of control or a thrown board. If that's not enough reason for you, climb cuts are usually not as clean as standard cuts.

You obviously have to be very careful with climb cuts. Take very light passes so you are able to maintain control. Luckily, there is no need to take more than a light cut. Once you've cut into the surface with a light climb cut, there is little danger of additional tear-out, and you can go back to a normal cut.

You must always be absolutely sure that you can maintain control over the board. Freehand climb cuts should only be done on workpieces well secured with clamps or in a vise, and the router needs to be stable and supported well. Exercise extreme care on a router table, and only climb cut on large pieces where there is no risk of the wood getting away from you, or of pulling your hand into the bit. And you should never make any cut where the wood will be trapped between the router bit and a fence.

Climb cutting

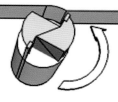

Bit rotation

Direction of router travel

The router bit cuts down into the surface of the wood as the router advances.

A shallow climb cut, on the right side of this board, avoids tearing out the wood below the cut (as seen at left). This can be followed up with a standard direction cut.

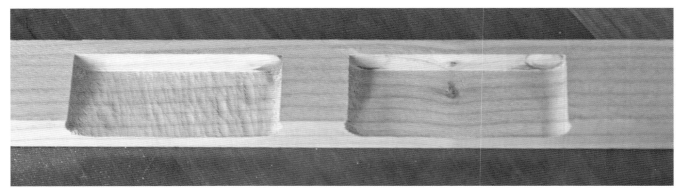

Fig. 4-105 - Overworking a routed cut (here, a couple of mortises have been sliced open) leaves predictably awful results (at left).

to best advantage.

But most of the time, the same issues arise; you need to maintain control over the tool while moving it in a controlled way. And this comes back to good body position (usually the basic woodworking stance), separation of force and control and keeping the work contained and close to your body.

Routing the edges of a board provides a good example. You need to maintain consistent downward pressure with your left hand so the router stays solidly on the work surface even though more than half of the tool is off the edge.

Your right hand is then responsible for holding the router tight to the work and transmitting forward movement from your lower body. (Fig. 4-106) More often than not, you'll have to maintain this control over the router as you walk along the edge of the work. Be sure to keep your arms in close to your body to retain upper body control, and use your lower body for most of the movement. You can also add a larger, asymmetrical base to the router to help with edge routing, especially with larger diameter router bits that will force the router even more off balance. (Fig. 4-107)

Fig. 4-106 - Routing is a familiar combination of lower body power and upper body control.

Router Safety

- Always wear eye, ear and lung protection when working with a router.
- Keep your hands on the handles and well clear of the router bit at all times. Routers can sometimes act unpredictably and your fingers should never be anywhere that they might be able to come into contact with the bit. Never hold the work with one hand while cutting with the other. Trim routers can be used with one hand in some circumstances, but you're better off with two hands on the machine at all times. There isn't much room for that second hand on the trim router, but putting a couple of fingers on the base – away from the bit – will help stabilize the tool. The wood must always be secured well.
- Router tables can actually be more dangerous than hand-held routers, because you've got much greater opportunity to get your fingers close to a router bit. Set up guards, and be aware that the router can pull a board in toward the bit, or throw it out away from the bit, with great ease. Take particular care when starting cuts, especially if there is no fence set up to help guide the work. You can run edges against ball-bearing-guided bits on the router table, but there's significant danger of the bit grabbing at the very beginning of the cut and throwing the end of the board into the cut instead of the edge. Starter pins or blocks – securely attached to the router table close to the router bit – will give you a point of contact before the wood touches the bit, and plenty of leverage to avoid trouble. (See Fig. 4-109, next page)
- Never run a board between a bit and the fence. The fence should always cover the bit.
- Never try to balance a full-size router on a narrow edge. You always need to feel that the machine (even a trim router) is secure and in no danger of tipping in use. If necessary, add support in the form of another, wider board clamped to the side of the one you're routing.
- Climb cuts should always be light cuts, with both hands on the tool and a well-secured workpiece.

The "L"-shaped platform clamped to the workpiece provides the router with a large, stable platform for routing this narrow board.

Fig. 4-107 - An offset base adds stability, especially when working with larger router bits.

Routing along or around a workpiece, you'll want to pay attention to the router's power cord. It can easily get in the way of a smooth cut. Putting the cord over your shoulder as you rout can help you keep it out of the way.

Other tasks have similar balances between control and movement. Plunge routing requires you to operate the plunge controls with your hands, control the downward pressure on the router for the plunge with your shoulders and upper body, and control your movement with your lower body. Router table work is much like table saw work, and requires balance and control as you feed the wood either along the fence or against the ball-bearing guide on the bit.

It's hardly possible to cover all of the uses for such a versatile tool. But it may help to list some of the more common uses, based on router type or common set-up.

A fixed-base router is commonly used for edge routing. This might include rabbeting an edge, cutting a decorative profile or trimming flush, depending on the choice of router bit. It is also useful for cutting dados or dovetailing when used in conjunction with an appropriate jig. Trim routers are small, fixed-base routers designed for smaller, detail work. The size and balance means they can be used effectively with one hand, although it often helps to add the other hand for stability. Trim routers should be used only with smaller-diameter router bits.

A plunge router can really do everything a fixed-base router can do and a great deal more. The plunge feature means you have control over vertical motion; the router

base stays firmly on the work surface throughout the plunge. This means you can move the router bit down into the work safely (this is not safe with a fixed-base router).

This allows you to cut mortises or other recesses in a board. It also means you can create stopped dados and grooves, or rout out grooves or recesses for inlay. A plunge router is often harder to adjust if mounted in a router table, however. Some newer plunge routers have added depth-adjustment capabilities that deal with this problem.

A router table turns a router into a type of small shaper. This allows work on pieces that would be otherwise difficult or too dangerous to rout. Router tables are great

Fig. 4-108 - Cutting with a bearing-guided bit in a router table. The starter pin provides a safe way to get the cut started, and avoids the tendency for the bit to catch on the end of the board.

Fig. 4-109 - Template guides (also called guide bushings) make the router even more versatile than it already is.

Fig. 4-110 - The router fence is another essential accessory.

for creating mouldings, raising panels, cutting joinery and more. The addition of a fence means you don't need to rely on the dictates of ball-bearing guided bits in choosing profile shapes or rabbet sizes. (Fig. 4-108)

Router capabilities can also be extended with some simple accessories. The most common of these are template guides and the router fence. (Fig. 4-109 & 4-110)

There's an almost endless amount of other work that can be done when using jigs to take advantage of the other basic capabilities of the router. It's usually just a question of controlling either the workpiece or the router.

Moving Beyond Basics

Once you understand the basics of how your tools work, you should be able to use them better and better, and exploit them in more and more ways. It's important that you learn the range of things your tools are capable of doing for you, and how to make them do those things. And you also need to learn the limits of what you can expect the tools to do. This requires a combination of experience with the tools, learning more about what they can do for you (by seeing what others have done) and learning to think differently about your tools.

If you think of your table saw as a rotating cutter past which you can move a workpiece in a secure way rather than just as a way to rip and crosscut, you may be able to think of ways to use the tool to solve different kinds of woodworking problems. You'll find it useful for all sorts of

things beyond its usual purpose. The same is true for all of your other tools. They perform basic functions, and cut the wood in a handful of ways. But those ways of cutting can often be controlled in other, less common ways. It may take some accessorizing, some jigs or some creative or unusual techniques, but this is how the tools become ever-more powerful extensions of your ability to create.

Don't be afraid to modify your tools to make them more useful. A hole drilled here or there in the miter guide or rip fence on your table saw may make all the difference when you set up a jig for a special task. It's OK to drill those holes (as long as you're not compromising some structure or drilling into some critical component). It's odd to say, but you have to develop a relationship with your tools. They have to become a part of your creative arsenal. And in a sense they all work together to become a larger tool that is your entire shop – a set of resources that solve all the usual problems, and that can also be turned to in order to solve all sorts of unique and different ones as well.

Your shop is a constantly growing and changing extension of your ability to create and to solve problems. Although you want your shop to have most of what you need to accomplish your goals, you want your goals to be growing and evolving as well. You can push capabilities further through more skilled use of the individual tools in your shop, through jigs and accessories, or ultimately, through new tool purchases. But never forget that it's the craftsman, not the tool, that has the skills.

CHAPTER FIVE

SHARPENING

A sharp handplane slicing through wood is one of the great pleasures of woodworking. Not only does this yield impossibly thin shavings and sensuously smooth surfaces, it even creates a unique sound, often described as the sound of a plane singing. After almost 30 years of woodworking, I still feel a sense of childlike delight at both the planing process and the results. But none of this occurs with a dull tool. Dull tools will compress wood fibers more before cutting them, and will tear some wood fibers rather than cutting them cleanly.

Without sharp tools, you'll have trouble getting acceptable results, it will take more effort to do your work and you'll be less safe.

Using a sharp tool is an essential part of woodworking. It is as much a part of successful hand tool use as the skills that need to be developed to use the tools. It is a threshold skill – if you can't sharpen, you're not going to get very far. And worse, you certainly won't enjoy the work.

It's not that hard to sharpen, yet many woodworkers are mystified by, or even fearful of the sharpening process. Given the conflicting information about how to do it, the many methods to choose from, and the supplies, accessories and tools to buy, it seems far more intimidating than it is. Sharpening is something that you should be able do in a couple of minutes max, without fear or hesitation. Once you've experienced a truly sharp edge, you'll understand why it's so important. Getting to the point where you can get a sharp edge without it being a chore is an important step toward farthering your craftsmanship.

So what is a sharp edge? There are two ways to look at it. Technically, a sharp edge is the meeting of two perfectly smooth surfaces as they come together at an angle. That's a mostly theoretical description. Our edge tools are typically made of steel, which has a crystalline structure. At a microscopic level, the surfaces aren't perfectly flat, and a perfect meeting of two perfect surfaces just isn't possible. Practically speaking, the surfaces are certainly flat enough, and we can get edges plenty sharp enough for our needs. This is also a perfectly appropriate mental model for sharpening. We need edges that come as close as possible to a perfect meeting of the two surfaces with no rounding over or crumbling of the intersection.

It's amazing how much of this you can actually see with decent lighting; rounding or crumbling of the edge (which is what happens when a sharp edge gets dull) shows up as a very thin line reflecting off the very tip of the edge. (Fig. 5-1) You just have to know what to look for. This reflection of the edge is one indication of a dull tool. But testing for sharpness is better done in other ways.

How you can tell if you've got a sharp edge? It is an

Fig. 5-1 - The bright line at the tip of this chisel highlights the dulled edge.

edge that is sharp enough to shave with, (done carefully on the back of your wrist or on your forearm, and not with narrow chisels), to cleanly slice a piece of paper, or to feel like it digs into a fingernail if you try to slide the blade forward with no pressure on the nail – if it slides forward on the fingernail the edge isn't sharp. (Fig. 5-2 & 5-3)

Getting an edge this sharp is not as complicated as it might seem, although it sometimes takes a bit of work. It all depends on what you start with. Steel is relatively easy to abrade (scratch) with particles of harder material. We need to abrade the cutting tool's surfaces enough to wear through any problems either in the surfaces or at the intersection, and then move from coarser through finer and

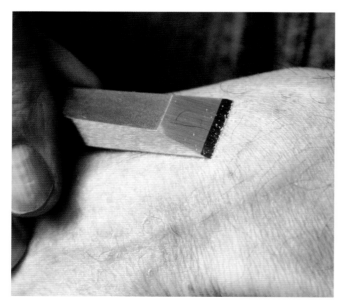
Fig. 5-2 - The back of my wrist is often shaved bare. I know my tools are sharp when I get to my forearms.

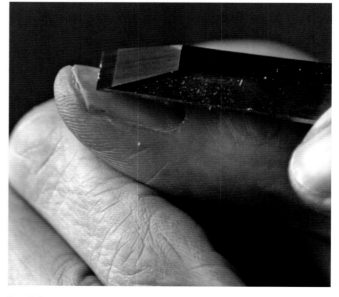
Fig. 5-3 - Trying to slide a chisel gently forward on the back of a nail is another good test of sharpness. Careful!

Fig. 5-4 - A set of Arkansas oil stones ranging through soft (coarse grit), hard (fine grit), black surgical (extra-fine), and translucent (extra, extra-fine). Photo courtesy of www.bestsharpeningstones.com.

finer grits of abrasive, to leave finer and finer scratches. This continues until the finest scratches are mostly inconsequential and the surfaces are polished smooth. The main issue is controlling the process to get the desired results.

Abrasives for sharpening woodworking tools come in many useful forms, each of which has distinct advantages and disadvantages. But unless you're dealing with certain specific types of steel, the choices are fairly simple. There are sharpening stones of various types, and there are certain types of sandpaper and sanding film, and there are loose or paste abrasives. For the most part, the decision is one of cost, convenience and speed.

Sharpening Stones

Sharpening stones come in two main varieties: oilstones, and waterstones. These are named, simply enough, after the lubricant you should use with the stone. Lubricants keep the stones from clogging up by floating away the swarf – the finely ground steel particles – along with any of the stone's abrasive that wears away. Oilstones are natural stones (typically India stones, Washita stones and soft and hard Arkansas stones). Oilstones wear slowly – they tend to stay relatively flat for a long time. On the down side they cut slowly as well, and they only come in a limited range of grits. They also require oil (a light oil, oil/

Grit Numbers

There are many different standards for grading the fineness of sharpening stones and other sharpening media. The most common is based on "screening" size – the number of holes per inch in a mesh used to sift the abrasive particles. In this system, the higher the number (the tighter the mesh), the finer the grit particles that sift through. But that's only one of the methods, and it's only used up to about #220 grit. Other standards from the United States, Europe and Japan all have slightly different numbering systems. But in general, the higher the number, the finer the stone. The one exception is micron grading. This is used for some sharpening papers and films, and is based on particle size. In this case, the smaller the number, the finer the grit (so 15 micron is coarser than 5 micron, and .5 micron is much finer than either).

kerosene mix, though some people use soapy water) as a lubricant, which is a little messier and harder to clean up than water. However the little bit of residual oil that tends to remain on the steel can act as a rust barrier.

A typical set of oilstones contains an India stone (usually a medium or fine grit) for doing the initial sharpening, and a hard or translucent Arkansas stone for the final honing. These stones are roughly the equivalent of a #240 to #360-grit waterstone and a #1,000 to #2,000-grit waterstone. (Fig. 5-4)

Waterstones can be either natural stones or more commonly, man-made 'stones' made from abrasive in a soft binder matrix that wears away fairly easily, revealing fresh abrasive. Waterstones (obviously) use water as a lubricant, and come in a wide range of grits, from #220 (very coarse) to #16,000 or even #32,000 (extremely fine). These stones tend to cut quickly; the matrix is designed to break down easily to expose fresh, sharp grit. This is both a plus and a minus; waterstones tend to wear down and don't stay flat for very long. They must be re-flattened often (after every couple of sharpenings is best), although this is very easy to do with either a diamond stone (see below) or with 220 sandpaper on a piece of glass or granite. A typical set of these stones would include #1,000-, #4,000- and #8,000-grit stones. The finer stones that are available definitely produce a higher level of polish (and a "better" edge), but only a subtle improvement in cut quality in wood. (Fig. 5-5)

Diamond Sharpening Plates

Diamond sharpening (or lapping) plates are sometimes called stones, but only because they are roughly the same shape, size and function as oil or waterstones. They are made by depositing diamond crystals in a matrix on a steel or steel and plastic base plate. These cut quickly, are sharp enough to easily flatten out either oilstones or waterstones and stay flat (if indeed they are flat to begin with). Water is the usual lubricant, which helps to float away the ground particles of steel. Diamond stones are not available in suitably fine grits for final honing for most woodworking tools, but are a great addition to the sharpening tool kit. They are great for flattening the backs of blades and flattening other sharpening stones. They are also good for many rough sharpening tasks, or as an intermediate stone between re-grinding and the final honing process. (Fig. 5-6)

Fig. 5-5 - Waterstones, from left: Medium (#4,000 grit), Coarse (#1,000 grit) and Fine (#8,000 grit). They are different sizes, and don't fit in the proper order between the strips screwed to my table.

Fig. 5-6 - These are examples of diamond "stones."

Fig. 5-7 - Here, I'm sticking some sharpening film to a granite reference plate.

Fig. 5-8 - Diamond paste usually comes in plastic syringes. Just a little does the trick.

Abrasive Papers and Films

The cost of a set of sharpening stones may be a deterrent to some beginners. Luckily, there is an alternative that produces excellent results for significantly less money – at least initially. Sandpaper is pretty common in grits up to #2,000 grit (try an auto parts store or a woodworking tools supplier rather than a hardware store for this). Special sanding films are also available in a different grading system down to .3 micron, which is about the equivalent of #12,000 grit. This film feels so smooth it's hard to believe that it is actually an abrasive, but it does cut the steel, and it leaves a highly-polished surface. The films are far flatter, and produce much better results than sandpaper, but they are harder to find and more expensive.

You stick the paper or film to a flat substrate (glass or granite are perfect, although other flat surfaces will work) and sharpen as you would on stones, using water as a lubricant. (Fig. 5-7) Pressure-sensitive backings are necessary to keep the abrasive paper or film secured to the substrate. Some people use spray adhesives, but these don't go on evenly, and typically leave the paper somewhat lumpy.

Another advantage is that you can wrap the paper or film around dowels or other shaped parts to help you sharpen curved edges on special tools.

Diamond Paste

Diamond grit suspended in a paste is also effective for sharpening. Diamond paste comes in a range of grits, with the most useful starting at 45 micron (coarse) ranging down to .5 micron (extremely fine). Squeezing a little bit of the paste onto an appropriate substrate effectively turns that substrate into a sharpening "stone." Appropriate substrates for the paste abrasive include a milled steel lapping plate, medium density fiberboard (MDF) or even a carefully flattened piece of hardwood. You can easily create custom, shaped substrates for shaped tools. Although the milled steel lapping plate can be cleaned between grits, if the substrate is MDF or wood, you'll want a separate piece for each grit. (Fig. 5-8)

The diamond paste cuts aggressively and quickly, and at the finer grits will take the steel to a very fine polish. You need to exercise care using softer substrates if a flat surface is important, however.

Grinders and Other Powered Sharpening Systems

If you're looking to remove a lot of steel in a hurry, there's a grinder out there somewhere for you. Grinders come in a bewildering array of sizes, types and styles, but the main idea is to move the abrasive past

Fig. 5-9 - This is a well-appointed bench grinder from Delta.

Fig. 5-10 - This is a simple, shop-made jig to help grind an even bevel on an edge tool. The jig slides along the tool rest.

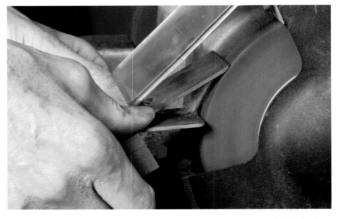

Fig. 5-11 - You can't really see it well, but the shop-made jig is in use here at the grinder.

the steel faster and more efficiently than you can by hand. (Fig. 5-9)

There are two downsides to removing a lot of steel in a hurry. The first is that you're removing a lot of steel in a hurry. This produces a lot of heat – enough heat to ruin the temper of an edge in an instant of inattention. Many tools will suffer if they get as hot as 300° Fahrenheit to 400°F, and the edge can easily get that hot long before you feel that temperature back where you would typically hold the tool while grinding. Water-cooled grinders are available, and these make it almost impossible to overheat a tool. Slow-speed grinders, and special, cooler-cutting abrasive wheels for regular grinders also make it less likely you'll overheat.

In all cases, you should be sure to maintain the cutting surface of your grinder by dressing the wheel often(using a special tool to clear away the worn surface of the wheel), to expose fresh, sharp abrasive particles that are not clogged up with steel particles. You'll need a wheel-dressing tool to do this; either a diamond wheel dresser or a "star" wheel dresser will work well. Also, slow down and quench the tool often in water to keep it cool.

The other downside is simply one of control. You want to maintain a straight edge and a specific bevel throughout the grinding process. This is certainly possible by hand (with practice), and there are a number of jigs that can help as well. A secure tool rest is key. There are plenty of jigs you can buy to help control the process, but even a simple L-shaped stop clamped to the bottom of the tool can register on the tool rest and help you shape a straight edge. (Fig. 5-10 & 5-11)

The trend lately has been to sell complete sharpening systems – powered grinders designed to apply the speed

Fig. 5-12 - The rounded back on this chisel shows up here in the uneven reflection near the tip. This is much easier to see if you move the chisel around a little.

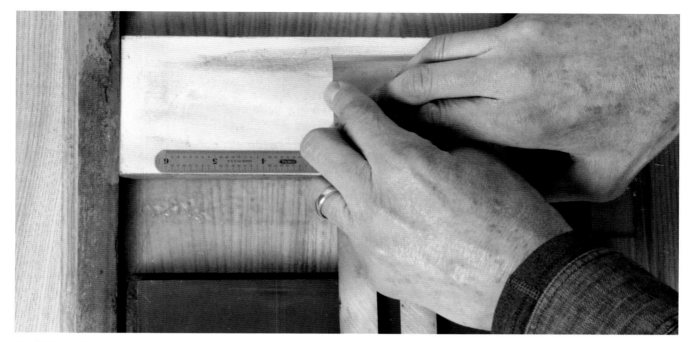

Fig. 5-13 - A thin ruler along the edge of the stone sets the angle for the back bevel.

of grinding to the whole sharpening process. These come with various jigs and tool holders to enable all sorts of controlled grinding and honing or buffing. It may appear easier and better than you could ever do by hand, but the truth of the matter is that in most cases, hand sharpening is just as quick and will generally yield sharper tools.

A grinder is certainly a useful tool when there is a lot of steel to remove. You might turn to a grinder when an edge needs a great deal of work because of damage, or when you want to create a new tool shape or change an existing one into something else. But for the bulk of day-to-day sharpening and even the majority of basic re-grinding (as in re-establishing the primary bevel on an edge tool) you can easily do without.

A Flat Back?

If you've looked into sharpening at all, you've probably heard that the backs of most tools need to be flattened and/or polished. This is where the sharpening process for a new tool typically begins. This makes sense. The back is one of the surfaces that needs to be smooth and flat as it meets the bevel.

Unfortunately this little bit of knowledge leads to quite a lot of trouble. A surprisingly large percentage of woodworkers spend time "flattening" or polishing the backs of their chisels or plane irons – only to round the backs over instead of flattening them. This leads to either a significantly less functional tool or a great deal of additional work. How does this happen? There are two main causes: by trying to flatten the back on something that is less than flat; or by flattening with poor technique. This usually in-

volves some degree of lifting up on the handle of the chisel or the top of the plane iron, or placing the tool down on the sharpening surface improperly. How do you know if your back isn't flat? Look at the back to see if you can see a reflection. The best test is to look at the reflection of a straight line (I look at the reflection of a fluorescent fixture). If the reflection is straight, you're all set. If you see the equivalent of a fun house mirror, the back is rounded over. (Fig. 5-12) This can be easier to see if you move the chisel around slightly while looking at the reflection.

Why are flat backs important? They're not at all essential for a sharp edge. Even a curved but smooth surface meeting another surface can be extremely sharp. But flat backs are critical for being able to control a chisel and certain other tools in many important cuts. A flat back means the chisel will behave in a very predictable way. Set up the right conditions, and you'll be able to make a straight cut. Add a little bit of rounding over on the back, and you really don't know where the chisel will cut – but it certainly won't cut straight. It also won't be able to pare off small amounts of wood in a controlled way. Relatively flat backs are also important on plane irons for establishing solid and continuous contact with a chip breaker, which backs up the blade and dampens vibration, thereby improving the cut. Of course, for this, the edge of the chip-breaker has to be flat as well.

But a completely flat back is not necessary on a plane iron. It is possible to create a small back bevel using a technique popularized by woodworker David Charlesworth, the "ruler trick." Place a narrow and thin 6" ruler (.02" thick) on the edge of a sharpening stone and set the back of the plane iron down so that the edge is about ½" from the other side of the stone. (Fig. 5-13) Rub back and forth, creating a small back bevel. Once this back bevel extends fully across the edge of the plane iron, you're done. You can now proceed to polish it by working through the grits up to an #8,000-grit stone or the equivalent. This creates a flat, polished surface for the purpose of sharpening but does not take nearly as much time or effort as flattening more of the back. (Fig. 5-14) And the small – less than 1° – bevel does not affect the performance of the plane at all, other than increasing the plane's effective cutting angle by a negligible amount. You will, however, need to use the ruler every time you remove the burr from the back of the plane iron in your regular sharpening process. You should definitely not use the ruler trick with chisels.

You don't need flat backs on carving tools, where a small bevel or round over is common on the back edge. The back bevel on these tools strengthens the edge (by creating a less acute and fragile angle at the cutting edge, while still preserving the shallow angle of the bevel) and allows for more control over cuts that aren't straight (sweeping into or out of a cut).

It is worth mentioning that flattening the back is pretty much a one-time effort. Once the back of a tool is flat you really shouldn't have to do this work again unless the tool is damaged in some way. That's not to say that you won't touch the back of the tool again; part of the honing process involves a couple of stokes of the back on your finest stone to remove a burr that forms on the edge.

Fig. 5-14 - The back bevel created by the "ruler trick" is the darker area near the edge. The uneven shape indicates that it would have been hard to flatten the back of this tool easily the traditional way.

Fig. 5-15 - Always put the tool down on the stone cutting-edge last when flattening the back. It's best to lift it off the stone cutting-edge first as well. Who knows if I'm lifting it off or putting it down here!

Important Reminders While Flattening the Back

- **Check the back frequently for evidence of rounding over. Look at the reflection of a straight line in the polished back – distortion at the edge equals rounding over – then check your technique for the cause of the problem.**
- **Make sure you never put the tool down cutting-edge first.**
- **Make sure you never lift up the back (handle end) of the tool.**
- **Keep your hands off the handle – it's best if you only touch the part of the tool that's over the stone, but you can wrap your little finger around the tool near the stone to assist in moving it back and forth.**
- **Keep even pressure only on the end of the tool that you're flattening, and pay attention to the feel of the tool on the abrasive surface.**
- **Use an appropriate lubricant. Not only does it aid the sharpening by floating away the particles of steel and grit, but it makes moving the tool easier as well.**

How to Flatten the Back of a Tool

Flattening the back of a tool may seem like a simple task, but it's actually as hard to do well as sharpening the bevel. It's a good idea to practice first with a tool that doesn't matter. If it doesn't go well, you're better off skipping this step for now rather than rounding over the back through a poor attempt at flattening. And you don't have to do this all at once. You don't want to spend so much time on a tool that needs a lot of work that you lose your concentration and cause more trouble for yourself. Better to do a little bit of focused work, then come back to it later when you're fresh.

Make sure the abrasive surface you use is flat and that the abrasive is very flat on that surface. Loose sandpaper on a piece of glass will not be flat enough, and spray adhesives are lumpy and should be avoided as well. Your best bets are a diamond stone or a piece of abrasive film on a piece of glass or granite reference plate. It is also possible to use a lapping plate (a milled steel plate that is usually softer than the tool) and loose or paste abrasives. If you want to use sharpening stones be sure to flatten them first, and then repeatedly flatten them throughout the process. Any wear in the stone will immediately translate into a rounded back.

Put your tool down on the sharpening surface carefully, with the front edge as the last thing to touch the stone. (Fig. 5-15) Then work the tool in and out on the stone at an angle. Keep even pressure on the end of the tool with both hands. (Fig. 5-16) One hand should provide most of the downward pressure; the other will help move the tool back and forth, while still pressing down. If the tool has a handle, avoid it. It's too easy to lift up slightly on the handle and round over the edge. Your upper body should be over the tool – a good indicator is to have your chin or neck aligned above your hands. Pay attention to the feel of the tool as it rests flat on the abrasive surface. You want to keep that feeling as you move the tool back and forth.

Fig. 5-16 - Arms in tight with your body over the tool is the right position for flattening the back.

The movement, as is often the case in woodworking, should come from the lower body. This way you're more able to maintain the control you need with your upper body. It helps to keep the movements rhythmic and consistent rather than random. It takes some downward pressure, but you're not trying to wear your way through the abrasive. Remember that working hard is not consistent with accurate results. When the time comes to lift up the tool, lift up the bevel first (by lowering the part of the tool that's not on the stone). This way you won't inadvertently round over the edge as you pick it up.

You're not trying to flatten and polish the entire back of the tool. It really only matters that you work the entire cutting edge. But trying to do too little of the back can lead to problems holding the tool and create "rounding errors."

Honing the Bevel

Honing the bevel is the day-to-day business of sharpening. And this is where sharpening's mystique is concentrated. Despite this, it is neither an arduous nor a complex process. It's hardly a cause for worry. In fact, it's probably the easiest part of sharpening, and is something that you should be able to master fairly quickly. Once you've set up a system for honing, you should be able to hone an edge in a matter of a minute or two without fuss.

Honing the bevel is a multi-step process for taking a slightly dull (and undamaged) tool, and restoring it to razor sharpness. All of the work (with a minor exception at the end) takes place on the beveled edge of the tool. Honing starts with a medium/fine abrasive (typically a #1,000-grit waterstone, a medium India stone, or some 15 micron abrasive film). The initial task is to remove enough steel to remove the worn edge. (Fig. 5-17) Once that happens, and

you reach the flat back of the tool, you will create a small burr all the way across the flat back edge. That is the sign that you can move on to the next-finer grit. You then work your way up through to your finest stone or grit, creating a smooth a surface as possible on the bevel.

Honing a Micro-bevel

You can save a great deal of time in sharpening by doing something on the main bevel that's akin to the "ruler trick" on the back of the blade. This secondary bevel is called a micro-bevel when it's on the bevel side of the edge. The micro-bevel is simply a small, slightly steeper bevel that you hone on the very edge of the tool. Adding a micro-bevel that is 2° to 5° steeper than the primary bevel saves significant sharpening time and can produce a slightly more durable edge. You save time because there's less material to remove; you don't have to do any work on the primary bevel. (Fig. 5-18) The edge will be more durable simply because more acute angles are more fragile (they do cut more easily, though).

The technique for adding this micro-bevel is different from that of the ruler trick, and often depends on whether you're sharpening by hand or using a sharpening jig, and then, on the individual jig. But the overall effect is the same in each case; you raise up the blade to a slightly higher angle before honing.

Over time, as you sharpen the micro-bevel repeatedly at that angle, it will continue to grow until it isn't so micro anymore. This means it will take longer and longer to sharpen, because you need to remove more and more material. It is then time to spend some time re-grinding the primary bevel, thereby shrinking the micro-bevel down to its proper size.

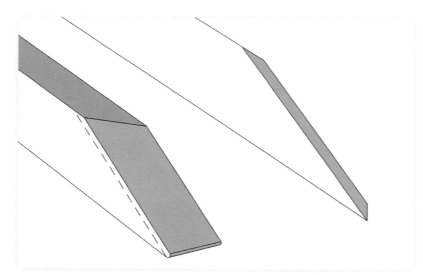

Fig. 5-17 - In order to sharpen a dull blade, enough material needs to be removed to get beyond the crumbled, rounded or damaged edge.

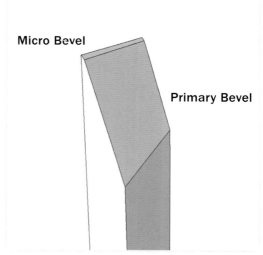

Micro Bevel

Primary Bevel

Fig. 5-18 - Sharpening with a micro-bevel means less sharpening (you're removing less metal).

Fixtures for Setting Up Your Sharpening Jigs

There are many ways to set up sharpening jigs for the proper angle. Some of the jigs come with angle setting devices. But it's pretty easy to make your own system for setting tools in the jigs properly. Most of the time it's just a matter of controlling the distance from the front of the jig to the end of the tool. And a set of stop blocks set the proper distance from the edge of a board will do the job perfectly. Deneb Puchalski, of Lie-Nielsen Toolworks designed an easily portable board that you can make. It holds a set of sharpening stones and has a series of stops set for the most common angles for sharpening. He even keeps a small, ⅛"-thick spacer attached to the jig with a string that can be used to set the proper distance for a micro-bevel when inserted between the end of the tool and one of the stops.

Setting the angle is simply a matter of setting the distance between the end of the jig and the end of the chisel. The blocks on my stone tray are set to specific distances to make this very quick and easy.

The four blocks at the near end of the jig establish the tool projections for plane irons and chisels at 25° and 30°. These particular blocks only work with one specific jig.

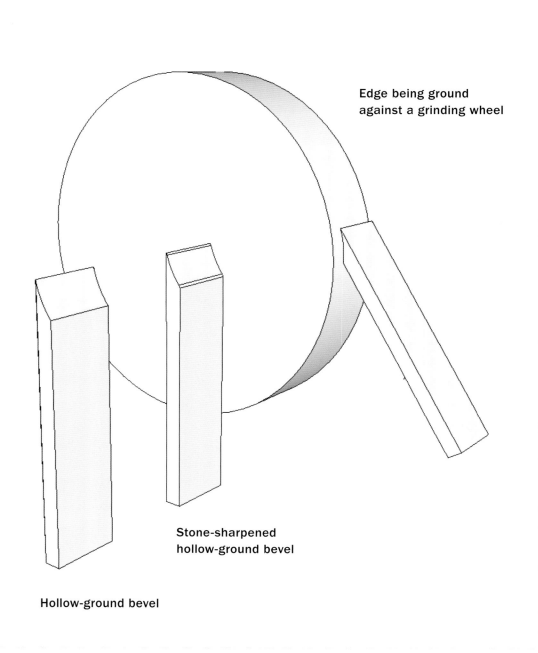

Edge being ground against a grinding wheel

Stone-sharpened hollow-ground bevel

Hollow-ground bevel

Fig. 5-19 - Grinding on the edge of a grindstone leaves a concave, or hollow-ground bevel. Honing the hollow-ground bevel on a sharpening stone leaves two flats: one at the front and one at the back of the beveled edge. There's no need to sharpen more than that.

Honing a Hollow-ground Edge

Some people prefer to sharpen with a hollow-ground edge. The end result is very similar to a micro bevel. This approach starts with grinding the main bevel on a grinding wheel. This produces a slightly concave edge that matches the curve of the grinding wheel. When you go to hone the bevel of this ground edge, you'll only be working the very tip and the very back of the bevel, because the part that has been ground hollow won't touch the stone at all. This is more stable if you're honing strictly by hand because there are two points of contact with the stone. It's not necessarily an advantage or a disadvantage; it's just different. Whether the angle winds up different from that of a micro-beveled edge is not a function of this technique. It's really up to you, because it's just a question of the grinding angle. (Fig. 5-19)

Setting Up A Sharpening Station

My sharpening station has a full range of sharpening options ready to go.

One of the most important things you can do to keep your tools sharp is to take the time to create a dedicated sharpening station in your shop. If there's room, it can be a completely dedicated area of the shop where everything is set up and ready to go any time you need to sharpen. (above) But you can also easily set up a portable, and easily stowed sharpening station that can be pulled out and ready to go at any moment. (below, left)

Why is this so important? Think about how likely you'll be to sharpen if you first have to clean off your bench, get out your stones, and find the appropriate sharpening jig before you can begin, and then have to put everything away afterward.

Make it easy. Create a permanent place for sharpen-

ing somewhere in your shop. It doesn't have to be big or fancy – just someplace where everything you need is organized and ready to use.

Access to water is ideal, but not really necessary. You can also keep your stones covered in water in plastic tubs (add just a touch of bleach once in a while to keep the water from scumming up), and spray just the right amount of water on either stones or sharpening film with a plant mister. (below, right)

Don't have a permanent place that will work? A portable set-up can be almost as effective. A simple tray will work (a lipped baking sheet is one good option). Store it somewhere easily accessible so you won't hesitate to pull it out when necessary.

I can also move my sharpening to a bench, with this stone tray based on the design by Deneb Puchalski of Lie-Nielsen Toolworks.

A pump spray bottle is an easy way to bring water to your sharpening station.

Sharpening by Hand

There are two arguments for sharpening by hand. First, it's faster. It removes whatever small barrier using a jig might pose; if you need to sharpen, you just go do it. And second, the control you learn translates well to other woodworking tasks and reinforces your fundamental skills. Sharpening strictly by hand is mostly a question of setting up your hands and your body to hold a particular angle throughout the sharpening process. It also involves learning to "feel the edge" as you sharpen, and the more you become aware of exactly how things feel as you work, the better. Don't worry if you're not comfortable with this approach, though. Jig sharpening works at least as well.

Hand position is critical when sharpening by hand. And a hollow-ground edge is helpful; it gives you two points of contact (at the front and back of the bevel) between the edge and the stone, but you don't have to hone the entire edge. You can also just hone a micro-bevel on a straight edge, although it's harder to keep a consistent angle entirely by hand.

Hold the sides of the blade with your thumb and forefinger up close to the edge. Place one or two fingers from the opposite hand right behind the bevel, and press the bevel against the sharpening stone. (Figs. 5-20 & 5-21) You should feel that you're supporting the tool well on the bevel. Don't hold the handle or the back of a blade (though it does help to wrap your pinky or pinky and ring finger under the tool). Your upper body should be positioned over the tool, and should be pretty much locked in position with elbows tight to the body. In order to move the tool without rocking or changing the angle, you'll need to rely on your lower body. The movement should come all the way from your toes. Only stroke the tool on the stone while moving forward. To bring the tool back you'll simply straighten your waist a small amount while shifting your upper body back with your legs. Then touch down again on the stone and repeat. Pay attention to how the tool feels on the stone, and on keeping your upper body locked and controlled.

Fig. 5-20 - You should be able to feel the bevel securely if you grip the edges of the blade you're sharpening on the sides.

Fig. 5-21 - Your other hand adds enough support to keep the bevel on the stone when sharpening. I would usually use more than one finger, but it makes it impossible to see anything.

Fig. 5-22 - Here is a collection of sharpening jigs. Each of them is good for certain jobs, but none of them is good for everything.

Sharpening Jigs

Dozens of different sharpening jigs are available to help you sharpen your tools. (Fig. 5-22) None of them is strictly necessary. It's quite possible to do most of your sharpening by hand. But it's worth pointing out that you're not going to sharpen better or more accurately by hand. You can sharpen faster that way once you get good at it. But sharpening jigs will always give you results that are at least equivalent to what you can get by hand, and will be more consistent as well. And you can speed up your jig sharpening with simple fixtures that make setting up and using a jig almost as fast as freehand sharpening.

Unfortunately, there are no all-purpose sharpening jigs. A jig that can effectively sharpen a plane iron is usually not as good at sharpening a ¼" chisel. Luckily, many of the jigs are not all that expensive, and having a few different ones around won't break the bank.

Sharpening with a jig should be done with both hands, using moderate pressure. As opposed to hand sharpening, where you only sharpen in one direction to avoid rounding over the edge as you move forward and back, you can keep the cutting edge on the stone as you move both forward and back. Keep your thumbs on the side or back of the jig,

with your other fingers applying even pressure over the tool. Your movements should be steady and even. Most of the movement comes from your shoulders; you don't have to limit your movement to the lower body as you would in hand sharpening; the jig will provide the control.(Fig. 5-23)

There is one less-than-obvious concern when using any sharpening jig. Be sure to wipe any grit off the jig (as well as the tool) when you switch from a coarser grit to a finer one. You don't want to transfer coarse grit particles to the finer stone or sandpaper.

Honing the Bevel

Start with a medium grit stone: #1,000 grit for a water-stone, a medium India stone if you're working with oil-stones, or 15 micron film if you've chosen the sharpening films. The goal is to hone the edge enough at this grit to create a very small burr that can be felt all the way across the cutting edge on the flat side of the tool. This burr is the sign that you have removed enough material to get through the dulled edge and have reached the back of the tool. This may take 10 passes on a tool that is in good shape, or many more passes on a duller tools. Switch to a finer grit (#4,000 grit waterstone, hard Arkansas, or

Fig. 5-23 - Here, I'm sharpening with a jig.

5-micron film) and repeat the process. You'll want to hone at this finer grit enough to remove the previous, deeper scratches; 10 to 15 passes will usually do it. Then repeat again, one final time with the finest grit (#8,000-grit waterstone, translucent Arkansas, or .5 or even .3 micron film). Again, 10 to 15 passes should be enough. Finally, remove the burr on the back with a few passes with the back of the tool flat on the stone (remember all of the flat-back techniques when doing this) on your finest stone or grit.

Grinding and Re-grinding of Edges

Once in a while you may have to re-grind a bevel. This is not all that different from the honing process, but in grinding you're looking to remove a lot more material, and there are different methods that are better suited to doing this coarser work more quickly.

Why would you need to re-grind? As mentioned above, if the micro-bevel gets too large, it's more efficient to grind the primary bevel, shrinking the micro-bevel back down to size. You may also need to re-grind if the tool sustains any damage: nicks in the edge; rounding over of the back etc. Or you may find an extremely dull tool that need to be reground just to get to a point where sharpening is possible. On rare occasion, you may even want to grind a tool to a different primary bevel angle for some special purpose: a lower bevel angle to make paring easier; a steeper angle to create a more durable edge; or a higher cutting angle on a bevel-up type plane.

Tools for the job fall into two categories: grinders or coarse abrasives on a flat surface. Which one you choose to grind or re-grind is really just a choice between speed and control.

Grinders are designed for the quick removal of steel. If you have the appropriate skills or jigs to feel comfortable with this speed, and its associated risks of burning the steel and keeping things straight, then grinding is an ideal method.

The simpler, lower-tech way to re-grind a bevel is to use coarse sandpaper on a flat surface in combination with some sort of sharpening jig. (Fig. 5-24) Self-adhesive roll sandpaper makes this task easiest. The substrate surface should be large and flat – a 6" by 24" piece of glass, granite, or even the cast iron table of one of your machines. The abrasive can be coarse (#120 or #150 grit) because the goal is getting rid of metal, not a polished surface. You can follow up with finer grits if you want, but if you're going to add a micro-bevel afterward anyhow, you can leave things pretty coarse. The newly ground surface will have nothing to do with the actual edge of the micro-bevel.

Sharpening looks more complicated on the page than it is in reality. If it still seems intimidating, buy an inexpensive chisel at a hardware store and play around with these techniques before you tackle a tool you'll worry about.

Fig. 5-24 - Here, I'm re-grinding an edge with #120- or #150-grit sandpaper on a chunk of granite. I'm using a jig to hold the blade, and the motion is the same as for sharpening.

SECTION TWO:

GETTING
A BETTER SENSE OF
WHERE YOU'RE GOING

CHAPTER SIX

MEASURING & MARKING

Once all of your planning and preparation is done, and you have a clear idea of where you're going with your project, you need to transform these plans into an actual piece. The transition from plans to reality starts with the layout process. Understanding this process and learning how to keep your project on track as you work is key to getting through the process successfully. However, this process is rarely as straightforward as it might seem.

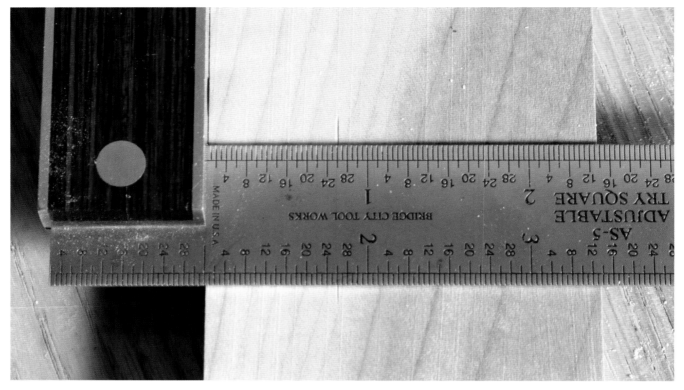

Fig. 6-1 - With eyes aligned, this measurement is $^{26}/_{32}"$ ($^{13}/_{16}"$)

One of the main elements of this process is getting away from a strict reliance on your rulers. You usually can't avoid the ruler completely, and "measure twice, cut once" is an excellent maxim for those situations. But you should remain wary of your ruler and the measurement process. Assume that any time you pick up your ruler, your chances of making a mistake automatically double.

This wary relationship with the ruler is a whole new way of thinking for many people, but the truth is, most accomplished woodworkers do not slavishly adhere to measurements. Woodworking is more than just translating mechanical drawings into exact and precise physical renderings. The process is more organic. There's a little bit of both sides of the brain involved. It's not that precision is lacking, but there's a great deal of nuance to that precision.

The Problem With Rulers

There really isn't anything wrong with rulers themselves – it's the very human tendency to make a wide variety of measurement mistakes that's the problem. It's hard to distinguish between tiny lines on the ruler, and easy to misinterpret even the bigger measurement lines (mistakenly reading $^{5}/_{16}"$ when the dimension is actually $^{7}/_{16}"$, or reading 23mm instead of 21mm). It takes a great deal of time to get comfortable with fractions (which most of us believed we would never in our lives really need), and keep sixteenths and thirty-seconds straight. There are mistakes

brought about by parallax, which is not having your eyes aligned directly above the lines on a ruler. (Figs. 6-1 & 6-2) There are mistakes caused by loose hooks on the ends of tape measures, or imprecise alignment of the ends of rulers. And there are mistakes that come from trying to correct that problem and taking measurements by using the 1" mark as your zero – forget to subtract 1" from the result and you've got "the inch mistake." (Fig. 6-3) There are also mistakes from manipulating dimensions, and all kinds of trouble with basic math and fractions.

There are certainly things you can do to minimize the most common mistakes. Familiarity will reduce basic misreading mistakes. Switching to the metric system (which most of us in the U.S. have not done) avoids a whole host of problems if you're not fluent with rulers and fractions. Thinner rulers have less potential to introduce parallax mistakes. Better-quality etching on higher-quality rulers makes it easier to distinguish individual markings.

But these don't really go far enough. What you need to do is avoid your ruler as much as possible. What can you do to minimize your use of rulers?

Existing Parts

Once a project is underway, you should use the work already done to generate sizes for related parts. And by this I don't mean measure and then cut to that measurement.

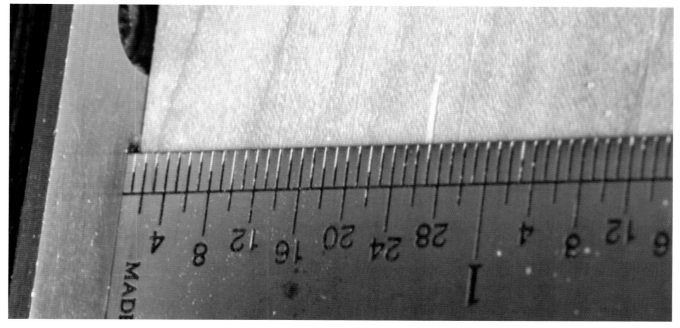

Fig. 6-2 - It's easy to read this as $^{27}/_{32}$" if your eyes are not aligned perfectly over the measurement line.

Rather, use one part to directly dimension another. Use the opening for a drawer in a cabinet to size the drawer components. Or use one part to directly mark the next piece to size for hand cutting or to set up a machine for subsequent cuts. You can also compare lengths, thicknesses and widths by feel with a much higher level of accuracy than you can visually (unless you're using calipers, which also work well).

Test Cuts in Scraps

Another way to increase precision is to make test cuts in pieces of scrap wood. This process allows you to verify dimensions accurately before you make any actual cuts. If a part needs to fit precisely between two others, make a test piece in scrap. Adjust the size if necessary. When you've got it just right, proceed with the actual cut. If you're cutting by hand, you can use the scrap to scribe a line for the

Fig. 6-3 - An inch mistake is ready to pounce.

Fig. 6-4 - With a complex piece, it's obvious that laying out directly from full-size drawings can be much more accurate. But this can help with simpler pieces, too.

actual cut, then either cut to the line or clean up to it with a plane. If you're cutting by machine, keep the setting from the successful test to make the actual cut.

Full-size Drawings

If you either have or have created a full-size drawings of a piece, you can use the drawing to create full size patterns, or even compare dimensions directly with the drawing. (Fig. 6-4)

This usually works best with moderately sized pieces, although full-scale drawings of complex larger pieces – or at least of details – can be extremely helpful as well. Of course, unless you're copying directly from an existing piece, you'll need your ruler as you draft the plans. The drawing provides you with a good way to verify that the dimensions are correct (you verified the drawings, right?); the drawing itself will reveal problems (as well as providing you with feedback on how the piece will look when you're done). Once drafted, the plans can provide dimensions, relative positions or can verify that your work is on track by comparing cut parts with the drawings.

Story Sticks and Patterns

One way to avoid your ruler – at least after the preparatory work is done – is to rely on a "story stick" for all of a project's dimensions. The story stick documents sizes, shapes and locations of the parts and joinery in various ways on a strip of wood. The story stick can be used as a direct reference for creating the parts as well. This is probably most appropriate for pieces that you make more than once, because the time and effort that go into creating the story stick won't necessarily pay you back right away. By the second or third time you re-visit the piece, you'll start reaping the rewards of that effort.

How does a story stick work? There are various approaches, and you can certainly improvise your own as well. A story stick for a cabinet might have the vertical elevation drawn full-size along one edge of a $\frac{1}{4}$"-thick, 4"-wide strip that's a little taller than the actual cabinet. (Fig. 6-5) The vertical elevation should be complete with moulding and joinery details. Horizontal dimensions, including details of vertical dividers, doors etc. can be marked out along the other edge of the stick. A story stick for a chair might have turning details drawn along an edge, along with all joinery details. Horizontal slats, rail shapes and other details would be drawn on the stick as well. There might even be notches in the edge so you can transfer locations of critical details to a rough-turned blank on the lathe. (Fig. 6-6) A small nail set into the edge of the story stick can even register the stick off the bottom of the turning blank. Accurate layout takes just seconds and is perfectly repeatable.

It's a good idea to mark the back of the story stick with the name of the project and the date (and perhaps a large "SAVE"). You don't want to toss it out with other scrap. It also helps to drill a hole in one end, so you can hang your story stick on the wall.

Patterns are pretty much the same thing, but work better with curved parts. A set of patterns can document all of the shapes and joinery details for a complex chair or other piece with curves. The main advantage is that the curves can be traced directly onto the wood from the patterns. And with a thin pattern, it's easy to refine those curves to exactly what you want.

Patterns can be made from ⅛" or ¼" plywood strips, or, even better, Plexiglas. With a clear pattern, you can pay close attention to wood grain choice on the parts as you lay them out (just be sure to check the reverse side of the board for wood grain "surprises"). Label patterns carefully if you think you'll need to use them again. You may not re-

Fig. 6-5 - Mario Rodriguez used a story stick while building this small cabinet.

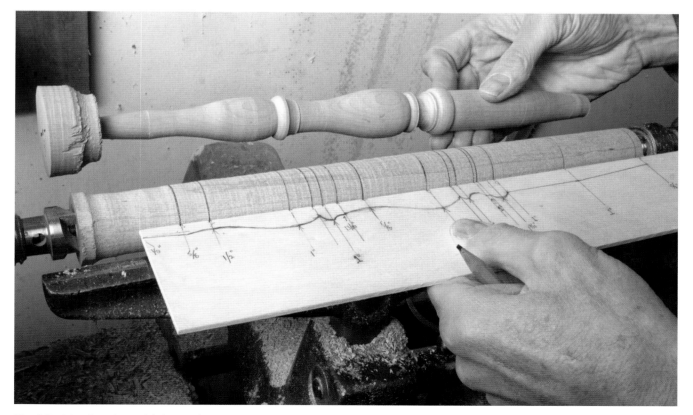

Fig. 6-6 - A turning story stick has a pin at one end to register at the end of the turning stock, notches for each of the turned features and measurement points, dimensions and a drawn profile showing what needs to be done. It saves huge amounts of time and leads to more accurate work.

member what they're for after a couple of years. (Fig. 6-7)

Avoid Unnecessary Layout

Your layout should be based on the context of your work method. If you're cutting all of your joints by hand, you'll probably have to lay out every joint carefully. But if you're using machines or jigs to help you cut or join the wood, it's likely that a full layout of every part is simply a waste of time. Once you've got a machine or jig set up to do a particular cut, it's set up for as many of those exact cuts as necessary.

Hand work relies on precise marks on every piece. The marks guide your cuts. But for machine work, you'll generally need to lay out only one part to help with the machine set-up. From then on, the machine set-up or jig will handle making the proper cut in the proper place. The remaining layout can just be in the form of quick pencil marks to help keep you oriented as to position, joinery location and part identity. And you don't need rulers or squares for these simple marks. The machine doesn't care, and neither should you.

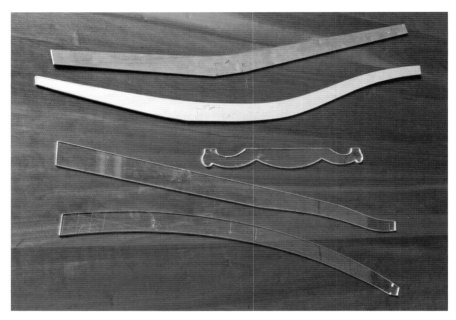

Fig. 6-7 - Patterns for various curved parts make layout much easier. The clear plastic ones allow you to make better grain choices, too.

Alternative Measuring Devices

There are also tools for accurate and repetitive measuring and marking that can make measuring and marking much easier.

Dial or digital calipers are an excellent choice for getting easy to read, accurate measurements. (Fig. 6-8) They are

Fig. 6-8 - Dial calipers take the guesswork out of precise measurement, but they can be overkill for many measurement tasks.

Fig. 6-9 - With their ability to mark clear, accurate, repeatable lines, marking gauges will change the way you work.

great for checking thickness, depth and the size of interior openings. It may be tempting to use calipers for as much as possible, but you should keep in mind that this level of accuracy is not required everywhere.

The marking gauge is an essential tool for hand tool woodworking, but it can be just as useful for machine woodworking. This tool gives you the ability to scribe precise layout lines a set distance from an edge. You'll find a wide variety of types and sizes of marking gauge. Versions with a knife or a cutting disk will be the most useful. A marking gauge can be set either with a ruler or it can measure and mark dimensions directly. Some versions can function as a depth gauge as well. A few even have micrometer-like adjustment mechanisms that make it easier to adjust and set the gauges very precisely; a big help. (Fig. 6-9)

Our reliance on precise rulers is a relatively new phenomenon in woodworking. Traditional layout was done with dividers. (Fig. 6-10) Dividers can transfer dimensions accurately, can be used for geometric constructions (accurate division of a line or angle in half, constructing perpendicular lines, drawing and dividing circles into segments, etc.) and are naturals for establishing proportional relationships in the design of a piece. A rectangle constructed with a 5:3 ratio is easy to lay out with dividers; just step off the right number of intervals on the two sides. Dividers are also ideal in the layout process for doing exactly what their name implies: dividing. This comes up often in dovetail layout, or any time you need even spacing of parts. But

Fig. 6-10 - Dividers make marking off equal divisions easy.

Fig. 6-11 - An adjustable square is a versatile tool. You can use it as a square, of course, but also as a depth gauge, and, as shown here, as a way to draw or scribe lines a set distance from an edge. Slide the pencil and square along the edge for a longer line.

certainly, other tools are better at marking or scribing lines.

Adjustable squares are very versatile tools and can help not only with checking for square. They are good at gauging depth, thickness or set-backs, and can then transfer these dimensions. They are also easy to set to a specific dimension, and can be used to mark out or scribe lines a set distance from an edge. (Fig. 6-11)

There are also dedicated layout squares, rulers and even protractors made by Incra, Pinnacle and others that are very useful. (Fig. 6-12) Most of these are machined to ac-

cept a .5mm mechanical pencil, which fits into accurately sized and located slots. These make accurate pencil layout down to $1/64$" easy, with no squinting or magnifying glass involved. This will still be not quite as accurate as a scribed line, but there are plenty of situations where it's precise enough.

Micro-adjustment With Shims

Making very small adjustments to either machine or hand-tool set-ups can be a challenge. The easiest solution is to

Fig. 6-13 - The Incra T-Rule has precision holes and slots sized for a .5mm pencil every 64th of an inch.

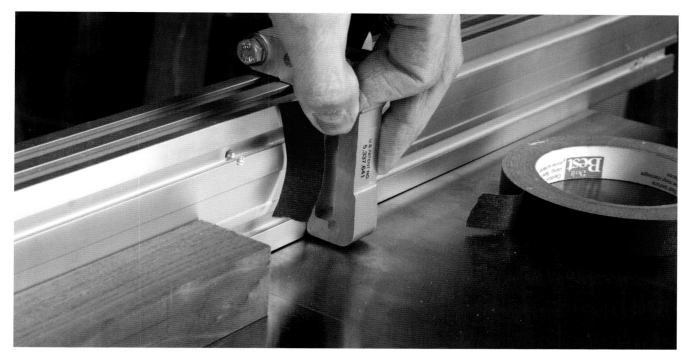

Fig. 6-13 - Tape shims are the answer. What was the question?

use tape or paper shims. This approach makes it surprisingly easy to adjust by increments as small as .001". Clear plastic packing tape is typically .001", 20-lb. paper is about .003" thick, paper money is .004" thick and masking tape is usually .005" thick. Some people use playing cards, but you'll have to measure them to get an exact thickness; they are typically .008" to .013" thick. Any of these can be used as needed, individually or in combination, to shift the workpiece or modify a stop or shim. This level of adjustment is very difficult with other methods. (Fig. 6-13)

Accuracy From Simple Jigs

If you need to do the same thing (either create an identical part or its mirror image) in different places in your project, you might want to consider making a jig of some sort. This can be a great help with either hand or machine work, and the jigs can sometimes be a simple as a rectangle of wood. For example, a plywood rectangle can be used as a jig to locate matching dados for drawer dividers or shelves on both the left and right sides of a cabinet at precisely the same height. In fact, if you start with a taller rectangle for the upper dividers, you can then cut down the same rectangle for the lower dividers.

You can locate joinery on symmetrical parts with a slightly more complicated jig. This is an excellent strategy for cutting the mortises on the two sides of a chair. Slots in the jig determine the location of the mortises, and dowels register the leg position. Pushing the dowels through the jig to the opposite side enables you to maintain all of the critical locations and dimension on the opposite chair leg.

The time spent on a simple jig can certainly pay for itself in accurate execution on even as little as a single pair of legs for a chair. (Fig. 6-14)

Build Accuracy Into Your Process

The more you look for opportunities to increase accuracy, the more you'll begin to see them. Make sure you design your process so you mill and then cut all parts that need to be the same size with the same set-up. Sometimes you can work on two or more parts at once. Cutting dados on both sides of a bookshelf with the two sides clamped together will – so long as everything is square – ensure alignment and eliminate transferring locations from one side to the other.

And Measure Twice...

When you do have to measure, measuring twice is a good idea. Even better, verify the dimension some other way in addition to the initial ruler measurement. And consider using your ruler to check and compare lengths more than to generate them. Rulers can also be used creatively to divide up lengths. (See "Dividing with a Ruler," page 147.)

Tolerances in Woodworking

One of the most confusing aspects of woodworking for both beginners and intermediates is that tolerances can be so variable. In a single piece of furniture, certain parts will be perfectly fine if they are within ½" of the "proper" dimension, whereas other parts may need to be within a thousandth of an inch or two in order to be acceptable.

Learning the difference between tolerance levels and where each is appropriate will lead to more accurate work. You'll also work faster, because you'll know where you do and where you don't have to fuss over microns.

Why are there loose tolerances at all? There are two main reasons. First is the nature of wood itself. If you're making a solid-wood table that's supposed to be 42" wide, this dimension will change from season to season as the wood expands and contracts. The table may only be 42" wide a couple times a year. It will be narrower in the drier season and wider in the wetter months. And second, it usually doesn't matter if the top is an exact size. An overhang will disguise any minor discrepancies (hidden underneath a top, even a ¼" difference from season to season will be virtually undetectable in a 2" overhang), and these will show up due to the seasonal changes in dimension no matter what.

Fitting a drawer or door into an opening (and numerous other tasks) requires a different level of precision. For the drawer, you have to create enough clearance for it to easily slide in and out of the opening, without excess sloppiness in the fit. The drawer also needs enough of an allowance at the top for the drawer to expand in the wetter months without binding in the case. If there are multiple drawers, the space on the sides of the drawers should be consistent and symmetrical. The same is true for doors; clearance needs to be both adequate for function and consistent in appearance between doors. The exact size of the gap is mostly a decision based on adequate clearance and design. It may vary from piece to piece, but you need an internal consistency.

Most joinery requires strict tolerances, both for functional and for visual reasons. In general, wood glues do not fill gaps with any strength, and the integrity of most joints requires a tight fit between surfaces. However, a joint that's too tight may split the wood as you try to fit it together. Additionally, a joint that's too tight may actually scrape almost all of the glue off the surfaces as it goes together. This creates a "glue-starved" joint (a joint with too little glue to effectively bind it together).

So joinery must fit together just right – neither too loose nor too tight. And the difference often comes down to a matter of a couple of thousandths of an inch. It's not necessary to keep micrometers or calipers on your bench as you fit joints, but you need to learn the look and especially the feel of a properly fit joint.

The basic rule for a mortise-and-tenon joint is that it should take a bit of a push to bring together, but anything that requires a large mallet and a lot of force or that squeaks loudly as you push it together is too tight and should be re-fit. A joint that takes no effort to disassemble or that falls apart on its own is definitely too loose.

Dovetail joints normally do need to be tapped together with a mallet, with gentle taps on each tail as the joint

Fig. 6-14 - This simple jig lets me rout two perfect mortises precisely (and repeatably) on both left and right chair legs. The registration dowels simply push through from one side to the other.

seats. Pay careful attention to the feedback of each tap; you want to feel the tail moving under each blow. You can usually hear, as well as feel, the difference when something is too tight. Tap beyond the point where the sound changes or you stop feeling movement and you'll split one or both of the boards. A few times through this process while paying careful attention, and you should figure out what works. It's a good idea to always use the same mallet or hammer when you do this. This consistency will help to you learn the feel even faster.

Even long-grain edge-joints, as in a tabletop made up out of a series of boards, need to fit within a certain tolerance. A good general rule is that a single clamp in the middle of the boards should be able to pull the top together so that the ends are tight as well (this is just to test the fit; many clamps should be used to actually glue up the top). This will work with either absolutely straight boards, or with "sprung" boards, which have a very slight gap in the center. Note that over a wider top you're limited in how much spring you can put into the boards; it gets harder and harder to pull gaps out as the top gets wider.

Start thinking of accuracy as a process that doesn't depend heavily on the ruler, and you'll go a long way toward doing more accurate work.

Dividing With a Ruler

Dividing up a space with a ruler is a two-step process. First, angle the ruler until you find a number easily divisible by the number of dividing lines you want (which will be one fewer than the number of divisions). Mark out the dividing lines...

...then bring those marks forward to the edge of the board.

Dividing a board into equal segments (commonly used for dovetail layout) is an argument to have at least one metric ruler around, even if you don't use the metric system for anything else. Hold your ruler at an angle with the end against one edge (or where you want to start the equal divisions). Look for a marking that will be easily divisible by the number of divisions you need (note that the number of divisions will be one less than the number of equal segments you're looking to create), and line up that marking against the other edge. Mark the locations of the divisions along the angle, then bring these marks forward to the edge of the board with a square. Note: If you're using this method to lay out dovetails on drawers, don't waste time and do this more than necessary. Transfer the marks from your initial layout from one part to another.

CHAPTER SEVEN

THE LINE

If you want to do precise work, you need to understand layout lines. Not only do you have to mark out accurate lines, you must also keep in mind exactly what you want to do with those lines, and understand exactly where you need to cut in relation to them. This varies according to the level of precision you need in a particular task (see the pervious section on tolerances in woodworking). In general, the more precise the line, the more likely it is that you will cut in the right place.

Fig. 7-1 - Sharpening a pencil with sandpaper creates a sharper point than can be achieved with a mechnical sharpener.

Pencil Lines

Pencil lines can be very useful in many different situations. Pencils are cheap and readily available. They make lines that are easy to see on most woods. Even on darker woods, where a typical pencil line might be almost invisible, a white or yellow pencil will make an easily visible and useful mark. Pencil lines are easy to correct and easy to clean up. Except in the coarsest woods, pencils don't tend to get pulled into grain lines as easily as a scribing knife or awl.

But pencil lines are generally the least precise lines you can make. The problem varies with the type of pencil you use. A plain old No. 2 pencil that you sharpen in a pencil sharpener will leave a line of a certain, indeterminate width. What's more, that width will change over the course of marking the line as the point wears away. How you hold the pencil can change the width of the line too. And

when the point gets dull, it will mark farther away from a straightedge or pattern.

It is possible to sharpen a pencil beyond what a pencil sharpener will do by sanding the point on some #220-grit or finer sandpaper. (Fig. 7-1) A drafting pencil "pointer" will also put a very fine point on 2mm drafting pencil lead. These will both create a very crisp, accurate line, but one that lasts only briefly before the point wears down and starts to draw a thicker line. If you're willing to re-sharpen often, this can be fine. Pencils are also available with a range of leads, and the point of a harder pencil (a 4H for example) may hold up better, but also mark a lighter line, and may even dent the wood slightly.

Mechanical pencils are much more consistent in the size line that they leave, but still mark a line of a certain width – typically .5mm or .7mm. Pencil lead is also available in

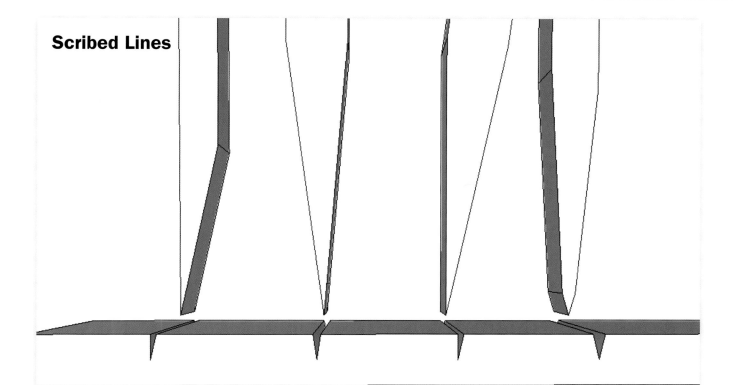

Scribed Lines

A single bevel knife cuts a line that's straight on one side and tapered on the other. The beveled side should be toward the waste side of the cut.

A double-bevel knife held up-right marks two beveled sides to the line.

Tip the double-bevel knife so that one face is verti-cal, and it's much more useful.

A knife with micro-bevels on both sides is a little harder to use. It's not as easy to tip so that one side is vertical.

Fig. 7-2

.3mm diameter, but it is harder to find (try an art or draft-ing supply store), and the lead is quite fragile.

There are plenty of situations where pencil lines – either ordinary or mechanical – are more than adequate for the task. You just need to avoid relying on an ordinary pencil line when air-tight accuracy is required. Pencil marks are perfect for rough layout, layout of curves, and layout of any parts that don't have tolerances tighter than the width of the line. Pencil marks are also fine for most band saw work, or any layout that will ultimately be cut on a machine where you can test the size or location before committing to a lot of cuts. You can also use pencil lines if you're plan-ning to "sneak up" on a perfect fit. This process of cutting, testing the fit and re-cutting until you've got the perfect size relies more on careful incremental cuts than it does on the exact location of the layout mark. And pencil lines are quick and easy in laying out either the pins or the tails – whichever you prefer to cut first – on dovetail joints. But the mating part needs to be marked out more precisely.

Scribed Lines

Some joints and some techniques require scribed lines. The most obvious advantage of a scribed line is precision. The most common tool for these lines is a marking knife, which will work well both with and across the grain. Dif-ferent people prefer either a single bevel (one straight side and one beveled side) or a double bevel (both sides bev-eled) for their marking knife, and for the most part, the choice is just one of preference. But there are actually two types of double-bevel knives: those with secondary bevels (these make up the majority) and those without. If there are secondary bevels, you'll have to angle the knife enough to allow the knife to cut right up against a straightedge. A double bevel knife without secondary bevels can be held at a lesser angle with the edge tight to a straightedge. (Fig. 7-2)

What is often less obvious about a knifed line is that the clean edge, especially if it is scribed with the proper side perpendicular to the surface, can become the finished edge

Fig. 7-3 - Marking across the grain is not recommended with a pointed marking gauge.

of the joint. Scribe a tenon shoulder perfectly, and that perfectly scribed line will become the finished edge of the shoulder once the rest of the waste is cut away. Thinking about joints this way is very helpful. Scribe the line perfectly and the rest of making the joint is just removing the wood up to that scribed line. This applies whether you use a marking knife or a knife-edged marking gauge.

Another approach to precision marking involves the use of a sharp pointed tool – either a stand-alone tool such as an awl, or a mortise or marking gauge. These tools won't will work well across the grain – a point cutting across the grain leaves ragged, torn fibers – but they do offer an alternative for marking hand-cut mortise-and-tenon joints or dovetails, where the marks are mostly with the grain. (Fig. 7-3) Traditional mortise gauges have two points that are a set distance apart, corresponding with the intended width of the mortise and thickness of the tenon (and the size of a specific mortise chisel). Both the mortise and tenon can be scribed, removing material inside the scribed lines for the mortise, and outside the lines for the tenon. A sharp pointed awl can also be used to mark out tails from the pins (or pins from the tails) in dovetail joints. These tools tend to leave slightly wider marks than a knife, but that can be an advantage because the wider marks easier to see.

The visibility of any scribed line can be improved if you run a pencil over it. A slightly dull "regular" pencil works best with a point-scribed line, whereas a mechanical pencil tends to work better on a knife-scribed line. Either will leave two pencil lines on the surface, with the scribed line indented in between. (Fig. 7-4) Concentrate on cutting away just one of the lines – the one on the waste side – and leaving the other line intact. Many people find that this defines the task more precisely than simply "cutting to the line."

It really doesn't matter what type of line you choose to make, as long as it helps you to understand exactly where you need to cut. In this way, the marking and the cutting should be seen as a single, extended process. If you know just where to cut based on your marks, the layout is successful.

This brings up the main issue with all lines: figuring out exactly where to cut in relation to them. And this is not intuitive. Keep in mind that any saw cut you make has a kerf of a certain width. That kerf should always be next to the layout line, not centered on it. Ideally, the near edge of the kerf just touches the line. This is easier to understand

Fig. 7-4 - Run a dull pencil over a scribed line to highlight both sides of the scribe. Try to cut away just one of the lines.

with scribed lines, because there is no real width to these. Pencil lines are a little more complicated. Some people talk about splitting the pencil line; others prefer cutting next to it, but just touching. The main rule is that you should never cut over the line. And that typically leads people to leave a bit of room between the cut and the line. Not only does this lead to more work cleaning up the cut later, it actually leads to less accurate cuts. This is because it's harder to cut a set distance away from the line, and to keep that distance consistent. You're better off cutting as close to the line as possible. (Fig. 7-5) This also helps to establish a uniform approach to cutting all of your lines so that all of your cuts (except rough cuts where speed is more the issue than any level of accuracy) are actually practice for the cuts that need to be accurate. And you do need to practice this; simply understanding where to cut is different indeed from being able to cut there.

Fig. 7-5 - Close is good.

CHAPTER EIGHT

FLAT, STRAIGHT & SQUARE

Most furniture requires that you maintain flat surfaces, straight lines and square corners, all intimately intertwined. Actually getting things flat, straight and square, though, is surprisingly difficult. The challenge comes from different issues at different stages of construction. Getting machines set up for perfectly straight or square cuts is actually pretty difficult (and may be almost impossible on some equipment). In addition, machines go out of adjustment, jigs get dropped, and even the best machines don't take into account user error, the accumulation of sawdust between the work and the fence, or the fact that wood constantly changes shape and dimension so easily, both as you cut it, and

after. And even square parts can be assembled out-of-square.

What is required is a systemic approach: maintaining a focus on flat, straight and square work from the basic set-up of your tools and throughout the process of building a piece of furniture.

This is not just a "do it right and you're done" sort of thing. You can straighten up an edge, and five minutes later, it's no longer straight. There's a constant process of adjustment, of constantly herding the project back toward acceptable tolerances. And even then, there will usually be some adjusting and compensating to be done at the end.

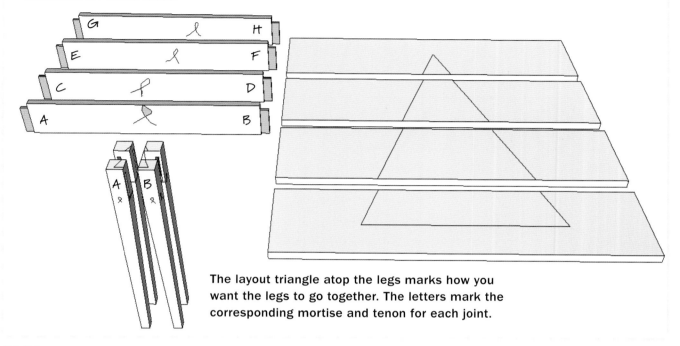

The squiggles mark the reference faces of the table aprons and legs. These should be the outside faces, and all measurements and jig set-ups should reference off these faces.

The layout triangle on the boards for a tabletop provides an easy way to mark the boards so their relative positions are obvious.

The layout triangle atop the legs marks how you want the legs to go together. The letters mark the corresponding mortise and tenon for each joint.

Fig. 8-1

Start Early and Start Small

It's only partially true in woodworking that if you take care of the small things, the bigger ones will take care of themselves. But the opposite is definitely true: if you don't take care of the small things, there isn't much hope that the big things will work out. Rather, things have a way of cascading further and further out of control as you go. Stay on top of as much as you can. It's likely you'll still have to compensate later for something or other, but it should be more manageable.

Keeping your project under control starts on a small scale; you need to start out with all of the individual pieces as flat, straight and square as possible. Aiming for straight and square right from the start is the best beginning to this project-wide undertaking.

Reference Faces and Edges

The first place to get a handle on straight and square is to work consistently from a reference face. Create a flat surface and mark it carefully. From that, you can then straighten and square an edge, make the other side parallel, and proceed onward. It helps throughout your project to keep consistent reference faces. All of the joinery should be marked from these faces, and any machining should reference off of them as well. For

example, frame-and-panel door parts should all reference off the outward-facing surfaces. Likewise, the outer faces of legs and aprons should be the reference faces. This way, joinery will yield well-aligned parts regardless of variations in thickness of individual boards, and outside faces will line up or have even setbacks throughout the project. (Fig. 8-1)

Tool Set-up

Even before you touch a piece of wood you need to think about flat, straight and square. You want to be able to do the best work with the tools you've got, and that may mean tuning them up and adjusting them to do the most accurate work possible. Keep in mind that the best way to check if your tools are set up well is to check the results. Don't just rely on setting up the machine or jig itself.

Flat

Flat comes first. It's hard to proceed with getting things either straight or square on a warped or crooked board. Your best bet is to mill every board yourself. If you face-joint and plane every board, you'll be reasonably sure of what you're using, and all subsequent steps will be easier. Unfortunately, this isn't always possible, especially if you're just starting out and lack the equipment (either the

Flattening A Board

1. Plane across the grain with the plane skewed

2. Plane on the diagonal

3. Plane the other diagonal

4. Plane with the grain

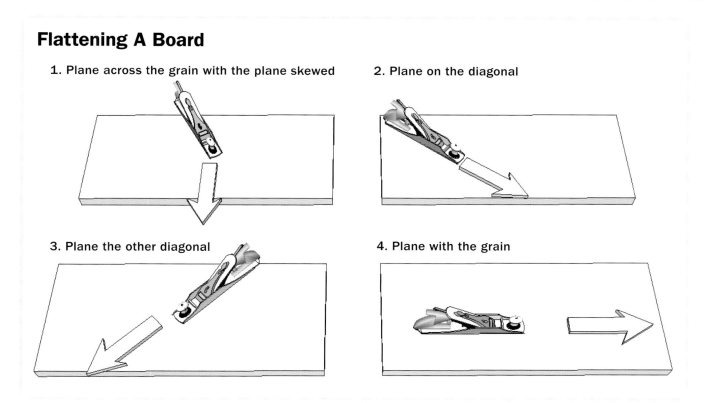

Fig. 8-2

hand tools or the machines). At the very least, you should sight down every board you purchase to see if it is fundamentally flat. The smaller the pieces you're cutting out of the board, the more minor variations you may be able to tolerate. And be sure your wood has a chance to acclimate to your shop before you work it.

There are usually specific parts of a project where flatness is especially important. Examples include rails and stiles for doors, boards for a top that can't be screwed down (as might be the case on a pedestal table), or parts that move in relation to other parts. In these cases, a process called "double milling" is a good idea. Double milling starts with milling your boards flat (jointing one face flat and then planing the opposite face parallel), but leaving them a bit oversized in all dimensions. You then sticker the wood (stack it up with thin strips of wood between boards to allow for even air circulation) and let it sit for a while, allowing it to move and adjust to its newly milled state. You then mill the wood flat again. The wood is then less likely to move much more, because you've given it some time to adjust. This still doesn't guarantee the wood will remain perfectly flat (wood is wood, after all), but it stacks the odds in your favor.

The best way to successfully glue up a flat panel out of narrower boards is to start with flat boards. A less-than-flat board may be flexible enough to be pulled into line as you glue up, but this introduces additional stress into the panel that makes it more likely to move later. Some of this may be inevitable; getting a whole pile of perfectly flat and straight boards to glue together into a tabletop is not easy. But it's a good goal, and the closer you come, the flatter and more stable the top is likely to be in the end.

Once a panel has been glued together, it will still need to be flattened. There are many ways to do this, from handplaning (first across the grain, then on the diagonals, and then finally smoothing or scraping the top with the grain) (Fig. 8-2) to running the top through a wide-belt sander. But even after the panel is together and flattened, it still may move around. This is the nature of wood, and quality solid-wood construction takes some of this into account. Appropriate fasteners pull tabletops down onto aprons, frames hold thin panels flat and dovetails secure case sides, bottoms and often tops, and keep them from moving around. These designs all evolved to deal with the natural behavior of wood in actual use. But even these measures don't always work perfectly, and there may still be additional work needed to compensate later (flattening out a frame-and-panel door, for example).

Straight

Straight comes next; you can't really cut a square end on a board that doesn't already have straight edges. There are many options for getting boards straight, and you'll need to have at least one available to you. You can't just rely on

Fig. 8-3 - The crosscut sled is a better way to cut square on the table saw.

buying straight boards because any time you do something to a board (including moving it into your shop) it may warp a little. You can straighten a board with a handplane, on the jointer, on the table saw using a jig designed for this kind of thing, or even with a router and simple router jig. The handplane (preferably a jointer plane) or the jointer are the most reliable tools for getting a straight edge and flat surface you'll be able to work with, assuming the tools and your skills are well-tuned. The table saw and router will work just fine with the appropriate jigs, but may leave a rougher surface in need of additional clean-up.

Square
The easiest way to cut square is with a tool or jig dedicated to the task. A carefully aligned chop saw works well. A crosscut sled for the table saw is more reliable than a miter guide (although the miter guide may work for smaller pieces). (Fig. 8-3) And a shooting board will square up

ends and give very fine control of length, while creating a perfect finish on the end of the board as well. (Fig. 8-4) A larger shooting board can even square up panels as necessary. Watch for interference from sawdust when setting up tools or jigs for squaring a board. That is one of the easiest ways to run into problems.

Once you've verified that all of the parts start out as square as possible, you can move on to the joinery. You'll need to pay a similar amount of attention to maintaining square throughout the joinery process. Make sure to verify that all tenon cheeks and shoulders are straight and square, that dovetails are cut squarely and to accurate and square baselines There's no way a case, frame or drawer will go together square if things are amiss with the joints.

Staying Square on a Bigger Scale
Later in the process of building your piece, your earlier efforts should pay off. But this is no time to slack off. The

Fig. 8-4 - A carefully made shooting board will give you perfectly square, finished ends, and allows you to adjust length by thousandths of an inch.

Fig. 8-5 - Be sure to check your work for square during the glue-up process. Measuring diagonals is the best way to do this.

glue-up process usually isn't complete without a check to see if the frame, case or drawer is square. Measuring diagonals (measuring and comparing the lengths of the two diagonals of any rectangular piece) – the best check for a square assembly – should become a natural part of every glue-up. (Fig. 8-5) And you need to know how to correct for problems. Angle the clamps in the same direction as the long diagonal to correct problems. (Fig. 8-6) You will usually hear a creak as the case shifts. Re-check and adjust again as necessary.

Be sure to level any casework before you start to fit either doors or drawers. The issue isn't so much that the case needs to be level, but that you need the case to be the same during the fitting process as it will be later when it's in use. Level provides an easy reference point – one that is both repeatable and likely desirable when the piece is actually done and in place.

After all of this effort, you would hope that everything would be perfect. But more often than not, you'll find

things are still off a little bit. And you'll have to decide if things are close enough as they are, or if you need to compensate still more. Sometimes, a little additional effort will pull things back to flat, straight or square. An extra table button and screw on a tabletop might flatten it back out just fine. A frame-and-panel door may need to be flattened out by planing or sanding the high surfaces. Drawers can sometimes be squared by inserting a well-squared bottom, or one that has been tweaked a little to force the drawer back to square. More rarely, a square case back can square a case.

Beyond this, you'll have to custom fit parts to openings. Plan on tweaking the edges of doors so the reveals are perfect all the way around, regardless of how square they are. The same may need to happen with drawers in their openings. Never assume that doors or drawers (or any other part) will be interchangeable. Everything should be fit to a specific location, and be marked accordingly. Consider this all to be standard procedure.

Fig. 8-6 - Adjust an out-of-square drawer (or case) by shifting the clamps on an angle in the general direction of the long diagonal (the long diagonal here was from near left to far right).

SECTION THREE:

LEARNING AS
YOU WORK

NINE

"A life spent making mistakes is not only more honorable, but more useful than a life spent doing nothing."

- George Bernard Shaw

MAKING
MISTAKES

What's your least favorite part of woodworking? No doubt it's making mistakes. Mistakes are costly in time, materials and self-confidence. What's more, our society frowns on failure, and most of us, for better or for worse, have internalized this aversion to messing things up. But in woodworking (and most other things), failure can create the most valuable lessons. Nobody wants to make mistakes. But you need to fail to learn important lessons. Naturally, you want to avoid safety mistakes – although we all will make some of those. The hope is that those errors will be minor and the lessons learned are both lasting and not costly. But ordinary woodworking mistakes are valuable in many different ways, if you learn from them.

Mistakes are not an inevitable part of woodworking. They're an inevitable part of being human. Everyone makes mistakes. This is something that you have to accept to get better. That's not to say that you shouldn't do something about it. You want to be able to avoid as many mistakes as possible.

This involves both learning and setting up systems for minimizing errors. It does not mean staying away from areas where you're likely to make mistakes. You can't get better without pushing your limits – and that means that you'll be working outside of your comfort zone, where mistakes are more likely. But if you're not trying new things and risking the occasional failure, you're not pushing yourself hard enough to make any real improvements.

Obviously, it's not simply making mistakes that is valuable. It's learning from the mistakes. You want to be sure you learn from as many as you can. How do you learn from your mistakes? The first thing to do is to figure out what led to the problem. What went wrong? Can you see the difference between your work and what you should be doing? Why is it different? And how can you change?

It's also helps to understand what type of mistake you made. This is important because you can use different strategies to reduce the likelihood of different types of mistakes.

We tend to make mistakes for a wide variety of reasons. But the mistakes can usually be categorized by overall type. Certainly, some people seem to have a talent for truly unusual mistakes. But even these weird mistakes usually (but not always – some are the product of true genius) fall into the same six categories. These categories are: mistakes of concept; process; execution; identity; measurement; and the final catch-all – carelessness or lack of attention.

Concept and process mistakes are the mistakes you make because you don't understand something. They're based on a lack of knowledge, although the knowledge is different for the two types. A concept mistake comes from not understanding the properties and behavior of the wood, how joinery works, or how the tools are supposed to work (things I've tried to cover at a basic level in earlier chapters of this book). A concept mistake might be a poor choice of joinery (a butt joint for a drawer front), a failure to take into account wood movement (gluing and screwing a solid-wood tabletop down to the aprons, or gluing a solid-wood panel into a door frame), It could also be using a tool in a way that splits the wood instead of cutting where you want.

Another way to look at concept mistakes takes us back to the "driving the car" analogy: Concept mistakes are mistakes due to lack of understanding of the rules of the road (driving the wrong way on a one-way street, not yielding the right of way), or a failure to understand the car itself (not knowing that you need to release the emergency brake, or that the car needs to be filled up with gas).

These are probably the easiest mistakes to avoid. Study. Learn. Increase your understanding of wood, joinery, tools, etc. Read as much as you can, and attend woodworking classes. This information is readily available from many different sources. You just need to understand how the knowledge applies in real woodworking situations, and then make the connections to the woodworking that you're doing.

Process mistakes are also based on a lack of knowledge. But lack of experience is really the prime ingredient. In other words, it's the lack of a more personal knowledge of

"Those who cannot remember the past are condemned to repeat it."

- George Santayana

what needs to happen and when. These can be sequence mistakes, or failing to understand how you're supposed to proceed and why you're supposed to proceed that way. Cutting all of the parts for a nightstand from the cutlist, then discovering later that the drawer is actually too small, may seem like a measurement error, but it's really a process mistake – the proper process would be to cut the parts for the drawer only after the drawer opening has been made. Similarly, fitting a door (or a drawer) into a case without squaring up the case first (and leveling it on the floor) can lead to a mis-fit door once the piece is together or in place.

The "driving the car" analogue would be taking wrong turns, or getting lost along the way.

Some of these mistakes can be avoided simply by seeing or reading about how someone else goes through the various steps involved in a particular project. But other things you'll just need to experience for yourself. In the case of driving, there are cases where a map or directions just don't reveal the subtleties of a complex route; you may have to drive it once or twice successfully to understand or you'll miss key turns along the way.

Building a piece involves a proper sequence of events, but sometimes it's hard to figure that out until you've made mistakes that show you various sequences that work, and others that don't.

Learning from process mistakes helps you to develop a better understanding of how you should (and shouldn't) get from one step to the next. You should strive to get a better mental picture of the entire process before you start. Think through what you're about to do, carefully scrutinize plans, and make up your own cutlist. Figure out how other people approach the process, but be sure to rely on your own experience as well. You may still miss a turn or two, but as in driving, you can always double back.

Execution mistakes are mistakes from poor skill. You know how to cut dovetails, you understand the layout and the proper sequence of events, but you still can't execute them. Your skill level is just not high enough to accurately cut or chisel precisely enough. Sometimes, this may also involve conceptual error; you may lack a clear concept of where to cut relative to the layout lines.

The analogy here is poor driving skills. You don't control the car well enough to keep it going straight down the road or to avoid accidents. You may need to work on the fundamentals of your technique, and then you need to practice enough that you can retain good technique as you cut more and more accurately. There really isn't a shortcut to the required discipline of practice. But you do need to understand what and how to practice (see chapter 11).

Cut a joint in the wrong side of a leg, or taper the front left leg when you needed to work with the back left leg, and you've made an identity mistake. The best way to reduce this kind of mistake is to try to get to know each part you're working on as a distinct item, and not just a piece of wood in a pile. Create a mental image of the whole piece and locate the part in the whole in its proper place. But even with a clear picture of where and how everything fits together, you should be sure to use a consistent system to mark each part for identity, location and orientation. Traditionally, layout triangles help keep things oriented and located; this only works if you get in the habit of referring to them. But any system you come up with and pay attention to throughout your project should work. You should also label all joints with unique marks (letter, numbers or your own personal hieroglyphics).

Another very common mistake is the measurement mistake. The most notorious of these is the "inch mistake." This is where you wind up with a part that's an inch off after measuring from the 1" mark on a tape measure to avoid the inaccuracy of the end of a tape measure, then forgetting to subtract an inch from your measurement. But there are countless other problems that come up as a result of inaccurate measurement. Inexact transfers of measurement and other small imprecisions are almost inevitable. Every time you pick up a ruler or a tape measure, you're greatly increasing your chances of making a mistake. What's the alternative? Don't measure so much. Rather than measuring one part at $33^{13}/_{32}$" long, and then trying to cut another that is the same dimension, use the first to set up a stop on a machine. You might also use the original to scribe a knife line on a new part, then cut to that line. Where it's appropriate, use scribed lines instead of pencil marks. With cleanly scribed line you're not trying to figure out where on a pencil line (of some indeterminate thickness) you're supposed to cut. There are plenty of times when a pencil line is accurate enough, but usually not when you're looking for absolute precision.

You can't always avoid measurement. And in those cases where you do have to measure, the old "measure twice, cut once" adage is a good rule. But that's just one way to verify measurements. Try measuring from a different reference point to see if that works to verify the dimension. In other words, if a shelf is supposed to be $11^1/_2$" high, how far down from the top should it be?

You can also start to think about measurements a little differently. Consider your ruler as an easy way to compare lengths, not necessarily as a way to generate them. Make a pencil mark on your ruler or tape measure to transfer a dimension from one piece to another. Rather than marking out centers by finding a length (or width) then dividing in half and marking out at the halfway point, add a verification step, and measure from both ends. The actual center will be either verified, or, more likely, centered between two marks that are slightly off.

Try to avoid marking out intervals by scooting your ruler along and measuring out a set distance from each new point. Each time you move the ruler, you can intro-

duce a bit of alignment error. It's far easier to use either the angled ruler trick (see chapter 6), or a set of dividers. If you do have to mark out intervals with the ruler or tape straight on an edge, you're better off keeping the ruler stationary and adding each interval carefully to the previous total. This increases the risk of math errors, so be sure to verify your layout from the other direction. Better yet, lay out two parts at once and reverse one as a check.

Carelessness and inattention can obviously lead to any of the mistakes above. These are probably the hardest mistakes to avoid. Mostly, they come from a failure to maintain concentration on what you're doing. This is no different when driving a car; distractions both internal and external can lead to all kinds of trouble.

It doesn't do much good to say that you need to concentrate more on what you're doing, even if that is the case. There are certain practical ways to avoid distractions, though. And there are also concrete ways to focus more on what you're doing. Ultimately, the level of attention you bring to your woodworking is going to determine just how far you can get, as well as how many mistakes you make.

Avoiding distractions is easier said than done. The obvious distractions – phone, family and work obligations, tool catalogs, etc. are bad enough. Some of the time, you may be able to find ways to hold them at bay (put up a "do not disturb" sign, turn off your phone…). Other distractions are even harder to control. Anger, frustration and other emotional distractions, as well as fatigue and pain are all internal, and can be even more ruinous to your concentration. If any of the above (or any others that I may have missed) distractions is strong enough to keep you from focusing fully on your work, you're probably better off avoiding your shop.

Mistakes in Plans

It's not uncommon to encounter mistakes in furniture plans. But this isn't something that you should panic about. You should always check calculations and dimensions as a routine part of understanding the project you're about to build. This is true whether it's your own design sketched on a napkin or someone else's printed plans. Don't start cutting wood before you have a thorough understanding of the parts and the construction. You should know the project as well as possible. And once the project is underway, you should work more from actual parts of the piece already cut or built than from the measurements on paper.

We all have our own strategies for immersing ourselves in our work. If you're at a loss for how to focus, try making up a list of very specific tasks you want to get through. It's also a great help to plan out as much as possible before you actually start the work. Try to build the piece in your head before you even touch a piece of wood. You can often accomplish much of this by drawing up the project (or at least, any complex parts of it) on your own – even if you already have plans available. Whether your drawing is just a chicken scrawl that only you understand or a three-dimensional computer rendering, the process of considering every part and every joint can help you to understand exactly where you are going. And this "road map" makes it easier to stay focused on the work.

There are other more practical rules for avoiding careless mistakes. Don't start anything at the end your work day that requires a lot of concentration (no glue-ups at 5 p.m.). Similarly, try not to interrupt (at the end of the day or otherwise) complicated layout or execution tasks. Once you've got focus, take advantage of it. And try to hold onto that focus just a little longer each time (see chapter 11).

Errors have a nasty way of cascading throughout a project, if you let them. This is especially true when working off of plans. Something goes wrong early on, and then you find yourself veering further and further from where you were hoping to be as you chase your mistakes. There are two approaches that can help with these chains of errors: Fight hard at the beginning to be sure you stay on track, or alternatively, let the project go where it seems to be going. If you have to get it right as originally planned, then you have to be disciplined enough to be sure you're on target right from the start. If that means re-making parts, then you've got to do that right from the start. On the other hand, it's a valuable skill to be able to build from what you've got. If the drawer was supposed to be a certain size and isn't, then build it to fit regardless. Try to get things to turn out well, even if they are different from what you intended (sort of like raising children). In other words, ask yourself if it was really a mistake, or did you just do something different from the plans?

Regardless of their inevitability and value, we all have plenty of motivation to avoid mistakes. And that motivation can pose a problem. But be wary of the paralysis that comes from the fear of making mistakes. Procrastination, in the form of endless reading, classes and setting up of the shop, followed by careful sharpening and tuning, followed by more of the same, is a sign of this paralysis. Your tools, shop and skills will never be perfect; and those are not usually the reason your work doesn't end up turning out as well as you might like. Most of the time you just need to do more work.

Making mistakes can be frustrating. And frustration can be the biggest barrier to learning from the mistakes. You

Highlighting Mistakes

Early in my career I hit upon the idea of fixing some mistakes (especially those in pieces that were for my house) in contrasting woods – highlighting them, in other words. I found this to be psychologically useful. First of all, I remembered those mistakes really well. It was also a semi-public acknowledgement that I made these mistakes. And I quickly started feeling better about them. I stopped – not making mistakes, but highlighting them – after a while. Instead, I've concentrated on fixing my mistakes quickly and (I hope) invisibly.

have a choice. You can channel that frustration into doing better the next time, or you can wind up too frustrated to do anything more. Make sure your frustration leads you to search for better work habits, more practice of skills, or whatever is necessary to actually learn something productive from your mistakes. There are two destructive alternatives: plowing ahead increasingly frustrated, which will lead to more, bigger, and potentially more dangerous mistakes; or just retreating in frustration and defeat. Rather than succumbing to either of these, take few moments after an error to calm down, then go back and examine the situation, figure out what went wrong, and either correct the mistake or replace the part. And do what needs to be done so you both remember the mistake and learn from it.

Admittedly, a constructive relationship with mistakes is hard to come by. One way to get a little more comfortable with them is to use an inexpensive (but still very workable) wood. Different parts of the country have different woods that fall into the "cheap but decent" category. Or you could choose a less-expensive grade of a better wood. This gets around the worry about messing up good wood. And if you don't mind quite as much messing up, you'll find yourself relaxing a bit in your work. This in turn, will encourage experimentation and maximize your learning. When your confidence improves to the level where you'd rather not waste time with the cheap stuff, it's a good time to switch to your choice of wood

Fixing Mistakes

There's an old saying that the pros are just better at fixing their mistakes. But that's not the whole story. The ability to recover quickly leads to greater confidence both in your everyday work, and as you push boundaries with new and challenging work. And this is how you get still better. Master fixing the errors (at least the ones that can be fixed), and you may discover a more positive attitude towards mistakes. Once you start to see fixing mistakes as just another problem-solving challenge, mistakes will no longer have quite the same stigma. You'll relax a little about making them, and you'll be freer to push into new territories where the real improvements in your woodworking take place.

The first step in fixing a mistake is to calm down. You won't accomplish anything effective if your emotions are running high. Take a break and walk away (unless you need to pull apart a glue-up gone wrong, in which case you need to act before the glue sets up), When you've calmed down a bit, come back and figure out what your options are. Evaluate all of the possible solutions, although you might want to re-consider any "fixes" involving a large hammer. Re-making parts is certainly an option you should

consider, but there are often easier or better strategies.

Here are a few easy fixes to get you started.

Patches

Patches can hide a range of sins, from misplaced joints or blown-out edges to defects in the wood. And patching strategies range from fitting small, custom patches to skinning over an entire side of a part. It depends on the situation, and how much work you're willing to do to save re-making the part.

One of the most important parts of patching a mistake is finding the right piece of wood for the job. Try not to toss off cuts or rippings from a project until the project is done. These are obviously the best sources for matching wood. Then pay attention to grain details. Matching grain orientation and direction is important. You should also compare grain-line density and color in both the part to be repaired

Beveled Patches

The easiest beveled patch can be made quickly with nothing more than a gouge and a good eye. Two angled cuts of the gouge around the defect will remove a football-shaped piece. Two more angled cuts in your patch material of basically the same shape and angle will create the patch. Check the fit, then glue it down. When the glue is dry, carefully plane, chisel or sand off the excess.

1 - Start to cut out a small mistake or defect with a gouge.

2 - A second gouge cut removes a football-shaped piece of wood.

3 - The patch comes out of a piece of well-matched wood, and is cut in exactly the same way as the defect. Don't lose the little football.

4 - Glue the patch in place.

5 - The result is an almost-invisible repair job.

Straight-sided Patches

To make a straight-sided patch, you should cut your patch first. Tack the patch down in place with a tiny daub of glue, then carefully scribe around the patch with a knife. Then pop off the patch with a razor blade or very thin knife. Rout out the recess with a trim router and a $^1/_{32}$" or $^1/_{16}$" router bit, coming close to, but not touching the scribed line. Clean up the edges of the recess to the line with chisels or gouges. And finally glue the patch in place and flush it off clean.

1 - Tack the patch in place with a tiny drop of glue, then trace around it carefully with a marking knife.

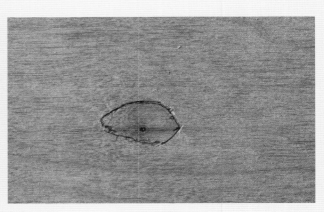

2 - I highlight the scribed line with a pencil to make it a little easier to see when routing.

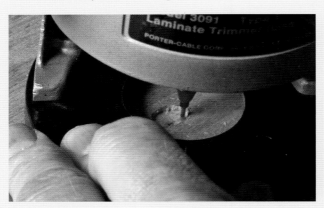

3 - Rout with a trim router or Dremel tool and a $^1/_{32}$" straight bit. Go as close to the lines as possible without going over. Clean up to the lines with gouges and chisels as necessary.

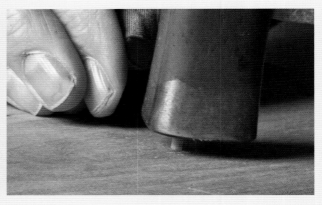

4 - Spread glue in the recess, then push or pound in the patch.

5 - Wipe off any excess glue.

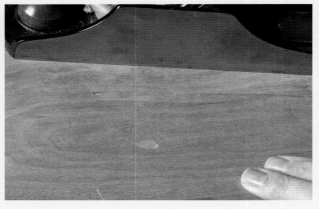

6 - The finished patch appears lighter here. But it was cut from the same wood, and over time it will darken to match.

and the wood for the patch. From there, it's mostly a question of shaping the parts appropriately.

There are two basic strategies for shaping and fitting custom patches: cutting either beveled patches and recesses (see "Beveled Patches" on page 169); or straight ones (see "Straight-sided Patches" at left). Both make excellent patches, although the beveled-patch technique sometimes gives you a little more leeway in your cut, and the bevels are better at hiding the glue lines. But it's also harder to do for larger, irregular patches unless you have some special tools.

You may be able to skin over a part after filling in an errant joint. Don't fill a mortise with a real tenon; you're better off making up a tenon-shaped piece with grain direction that matches the part.

Out-of-square Cases or Drawers

Oops. The drawer comes out of clamps and you've forgotten to square it up. It's a little bit more like a parallelogram than a rectangle. There is a chance to save it. Often, a closely fit and square plywood drawer bottom slid into place will help pull things back to square. The trick is to pull the drawer back into line with a clamp while you slide the bottom in place, and then attach it to the back of the drawer at the back. This won't work with a solid-wood drawer bottom, because you need to leave room for expansion and contraction. You may also be able to install a drawer bottom that's out of square in the opposite direction to "persuade" the drawer a bit more. Similar techniques will sometimes work with out-of-square cases.

Shop Rash

Shop rash is the collective name (in my shop, at least) for the dings and dents that seem to crop up on a project over the course of construction. These dents and dings aren't really mistakes, but are almost the almost inevitable consequence of working on a project. But you can also look at them as process errors. They come from a poor system for handling parts and inadequate padding and protection of your work as you build it and move it around in the shop.

There are a few rules for minimizing shop rash.

- Always have a plentiful supply of either shop-made or purchased clamp pads available, and use them.
- Keep moving blankets or other pads handy, and use them. These can also be used as workbench pads, or you can have other workbench padding available (carpet scraps, foam, exercise mats, etc).
- Never leave something standing upright. If there's any chance it might fall over, it probably will.
- And finally, pay attention to process, and do final smoothing as late in the project as possible (for example, just before assembly), so you don't leave finished surfaces at risk while other parts of the piece still need work.

Fixing Tenons

Tenons that are too small for their mortises can sometimes be salvaged with a patch glued to one of the cheeks. The patch can be either a thin piece of solid wood or a slice of veneer. In either case, glue the patch down using a block of wood as a caul. Then re-fit the tenon properly. Keep in mind The patch does not structurally restore the thickness or the strength of the tenon; if you put a $\frac{1}{8}$" thick patch on a tenon that is $\frac{1}{4}$" thick to fit it into a $\frac{3}{8}$"-wide mortise, the tenon only has the strength of a $\frac{1}{4}$" tenon. It will now fit the mortise, and the glue joint will be strong, but you'll need to decide if the joint will be able to handle the stress or the load in your piece.

1 -Start patching a tenon that's too small for its mortise by gluing a patch onto the tenon. Spread the glue...

2 ...put the patch in place...

3 ...and clamp it in place, using a small block of wood as a caul to distribute the pressure. Re-fit the tenon when the glue is dry.

CHAPTER TEN

FEEDBACK

One of the best ways to improve your woodworking skills is to pay more attention to the feedback you get as you work. Certainly, you're already paying attention to the quality of the overall work. You look at what you've done with some mixture of pride and chagrin based on how it turned out. Or you seek out comments from someone else, which can be even more valuable. If you find someone willing and capable of looking at your work with a critical and helpful eye, you may be surprised by how much more that person sees in your work and your designs than you were aware of. This takes a certain amount of courage, of course, but the payoff is almost certainly worth it. You will be able to see your work more clearly, and will have a far better idea of what you need to improve. The simple truth is that knowing where you need to go in your work plays a crucial role in getting there.

This type of feedback certainly motivates you to do better. But the way to actually get better involves different types of feedback. These types of feedback come from a wide variety of sources as you do the work. And many people operate without this feedback loop altogether.

Rather than waiting until the end to assess what happened with your project, you want to get feedback at every step of the way. Every cut, every stroke of a handplane, even every pass with a piece of sandpaper does something to the wood, and you need to know just what the result is in order to gain greater control of the process. I'm not suggesting that you stop to examine the result of every move you make, but you should certainly be aware of the consequences of everything you do. Are your edges straight? Are the cuts square? Are the cut edges smooth? As you work to fit a tenon, are you tapering it in one direction or another? Are you leaving cross-grain or diagonal scratches in the wood with sandpaper, or rounding over the edges or even the surfaces? What does it mean to your project if things are going astray at this level? Thinking about each of these factors as you work shouldn't be a chore; it's just a part of being fully engaged in your work. The more you do it, the more of this information you'll start to pick up. With more immediate feedback you'll be able to steer the project closer to your goals. What happens if you shorten up the feedback loop even more? Strive to pay attention to all of the sensations – what you feel, see, hear and even smell – while you work, and you'll begin doing just that. And as you do this more and more, you'll become aware of another level of subtle but important signals that can keep your work heading in the right direction. The ability to benefit from these signals relies on much of what you've learned about wood and your tools. You need to understand your tools, processes and the nature of your material in order to have the sights, sounds and tactile responses you encounter make sense. The feedback reinforces your knowledge in very practical ways. One example: A router runs noisier when it's being pushed too hard because the router bit is struggling to make the cut. The bit chatters and cuts a rougher and slightly wider path. Once you're aware of that and paying attention to the sound, you can easily minimize these lesser-quality cuts.

That is an example of a negative feedback; the sound indicates a problem. There is also positive feedback. Cut with a sharp and well-tuned handplane, and you'll hear a particular sound that tells you all is well with the cut and the plane. Chisels, too, will proclaim their keen edges with a unique sound (mostly heard when paring end grain). If you don't hear these sounds, you'll know that the sharp edge is beginning to break down. It doesn't necessarily mean you need to sharpen right away, but it's certainly a sign that you need to sharpen soon.

Visual Feedback

It seems obvious that you should watch what you're doing more closely, but it's surprising how rarely people do it. The more you learn to observe, the more "signals" you will have to help stay on track to do your work more accurately.

You also need to learn what to watch. You need to pay attention to different things in different situations. For example, when using hand tools, it is often more important to pay attention to the workpiece than to watch yourself doing the work. In other words, looking at the results of what you're doing, and not at the process, is more important to monitoring your work. But there are times when it's important to watch yourself work as well. Sighting down the edge of a chisel (with your dominant eye) will give you the best sense of a straight and square cut. Monitoring the shavings coming out of the mouth of a handplane is also valuable, at least during the set-up process. If the shaving is not coming off the board evenly it's telling you something. Is the plane adjusted correctly? Are you holding the tool at an angle? Once you've checked your plane (and checked to see if you're centered on the board), you'll know to pay attention any "lean" you might be putting into your planing. It's still important to be aware of the results of every stroke of the handplane. Even with a well-adjusted plane, you don't want to just scrub away for a while before you finally check what you've actually done. The feedback here will teach you just how much you actually remove in each pass, or in five or 10 passes. You'll get a better sense of what your plane is doing.

Power tools can be a little different. It is usually more important to focus on various control and safety points. Proper ripping on a table saw involves keeping a board tight against the fence and being sure your hand position is safe. You certainly need to be aware of the guard, the blade and your proximity to it, but watching the actual cut won't accomplish much; the other factors have far more control over the quality of the cut and your overall safety. Watch the board and its contact with the fence, instead.

To enhance other types of visual feedback, you may need to look at your work in a different way. A low light source can reveal scribed lines and surface defects that might otherwise be invisible. And viewing your work at a different angle can reveal a lot that can't otherwise be seen easily. Combine both the low angle and a low, raking light source and you'll see even more.

An even more important concept is to be sure you set up yourself, your work, and your lighting so you can use your eyes to best advantage at all times. Be sure you can see what needs to be seen. For example, if you need to be sure that you're paring something square, you want to be sure that you and the work are in a position where you can see that the chisel is square to the work. If you're cutting to a line, you, the tool, the work and the lighting should be arranged so you can always see the relationship between tool and line. This requires a bit of thought when you first start out, and it may mean moving yourself, your workpiece and perhaps your lights around a little more than you're used to. You'll get used to it, and the end result of being able to see crucial details and relationships will be greater accuracy.

Tactile Feedback

Your sense of touch is remarkably sensitive; it can detect variations as small as a thousandth of an inch. Combine this sensitivity with the motion of your hand or fingers and you'll find you can feel minute variations in a surface or edge that are much too small to see (at least before the finish goes on). Don't just use one finger in motion; use three or four when you test out an edge, or your whole hand when checking a surface. You'll pick up much more information that way. But that's just the beginning of what your sense of touch will tell you. Tactile feedback will be your primary source of information as you dynamically change the pressure you apply to a handplane. And sensitivity to vibration will help you adjust the speed at which

you feed stock into a machine or move either a hand or power tool over a workpiece.

Your tactile sense of pressure is important for maintaining a tool flat on a surface throughout a movement. This can help keep a plane oriented flat on an edge (even a curved one), or the back of a chisel flat on a sharpening stone during flattening. In general, paying attention to every aspect – the feel of a tool in your hands as it cuts (pressure, vibration, movement, and sometimes, even temperature) – provides you with information that will help you to use the tool better.

Audible Feedback

Maybe it's my former training as a musician, but I always found the sounds of the shop both intriguing and informative. In my shop, both during classes and during regular work, I monitor what's going on by sound as much as I do by sight. The sounds can tell me how someone is doing with either hand or power tools. You can learn to hear when your own (or someone else's) work is tense, tentative, or overly aggressive, or if everything is going well. And you can usually tell by sound alone if a tool is being

Specific feedback and what it might indicate

Visual:
- Learn to see more in the wood – subtle marks from machines (ripples from the planer or router bits, saw marks), or from hand tools (the quality of the blade, any blade chatter).
- Look for things revealed in different types of light, especially from a low-angle raking light – in particular, scribed lines that might be invisible under full light.
- Watch the interface between machined wood and planed wood to ensure you're staying square (this works most obviously with a bandsawn edge, but can also be used with a tablesawn edge).

Audible:
- The sound of a plane, scraper, or even sandpaper can reveal the marks left by a jointer or planer on a board's edge or surface
- The sound of a well-sharpened plane or chisel
- You can tell when a handsaw is being used with a good balance of speed and pressure; a relaxed stroke vs. a tense one.
- You can tell if you're going with or against the grain with a handplane, jointer or planer (listen for the crackle of the fibers tearing out).

Tactile:
- Check a curved surface to determine if it is smooth.
- Feel a large flat surface for variations that won't turn up until the finish is on.
- Feel for a chisel edge fitting into a scribed line.

Olfactory:
- Enjoy the smells of different woods.
- Pick up on burning during a cut, or the smell of overheating machines (burning lubricant), electrical problems (the smell of ozone).
- Checking the fit and quality of a dust mask (you shouldn't be able to smell the wood)

Integrated senses:
- Determine if a machine is being overworked as it cuts (excess vibration and chatter, machine sounds slower).
- Decide if a machine needs attention (bad bearings, poor mechanical alignment, parts rubbing, feeling vibration, hearing odd, louder or changed sounds, smelling the burning the wood).

overworked or used improperly. If you're listening well, you can even hear some basic measures of quality. A complete pass over the edge or surface of a board on the jointer sounds different than one that misses a spot or two. You can sometimes hear any remaining machine marks on a board as you work it with hand tools, even if you can't quite see them. And you can hear otherwise invisible cracks or hollow areas in a workpiece when you're moving your hands or tools over them.

Olfactory Feedback?

Even smell can tell you things, although there aren't too many that are as helpful to quality woodworking as the other senses can provide. The smell will let you know when you're burning the wood because of either a dull tool or too slow a feed rate. Smell also lets you know when you forgot to turn on the dust collector, but that rarely affects the work as much as the cleanup, or ultimately your respiratory health.

Putting all of Your Senses to Work Together

Your senses don't operate in isolation in the real world. And even with hearing protection, you're not shutting off your ability to glean information from the sounds of the shop. All of your senses work together to provide you with a rich stream of feedback.

Try this out on your table saw: Make a set of three crosscuts on a roughly 3"-wide, ¾"-thick piece of scrap (cherry is good for this. Make one cut very slowly (more than three seconds for the complete crosscut), one cut very quickly (less than half a second) and one at a pace in the middle. Listen to the cuts, and pay attention to how they feel. You can even pay attention to how they smell! Now examine the results. If you're pushing through too slowly, you may find burn marks on the end grain of the cut. A pass that's too quick will look ragged; the fibers have been ripped out of the board, because the teeth on the blade didn't have a chance to cut cleanly. Assuming you have a decent blade, a "just right" cut will be smooth and clean, with no burn marks (or burnt smell). Get used to all of the sensations of the just-right cut, and you'll automatically adjust to get that feeling more and more often.

Slow Down

It's difficult to suddenly start paying attention to so many things all at once. But little by little, you should start making these associations a part of your everyday woodworking. Go slowly at first. This means actually taking your time, so you have time to pay attention to the feedback. Although this doesn't work as well with machines where going too slowly can burn the wood, you'll find the experience with hand tools revealing as you slow down. Certainly, some things are harder to do slowly. You'll be forced to pay attention to proper use of the rest of your body (this is a good way to see if you're using your body well). And you'll be able to feel more of what you're doing to the wood. Try to keep the awareness of all of the feedback the same as you speed up again. As you then adjust your woodworking to what you hear, see and feel, you'll be much quicker and surer on your path toward quality. It may seem daunting at first, but you'll find that greater awareness will quickly become a part of your work habits.

Here, you can see the typical results of cuts that are, from bottom to top, too fast, too slow and just right.

ELEVEN

PRACTICING

You can't learn how to ride a bicycle by reading about it. You can't learn woodworking by just reading about it, either. It's not all theoretical knowledge. Woodworking needs to be experienced, felt and learned in the muscles (or the neurological connections). And sadly, woodworking is not like riding a bicycle in that you never forget.

In order to master certain skills in woodworking you're going to have to practice more than you might think. Much of this stuff just does not come naturally, even to the most gifted woodworkers. The original system by which woodworking was both taught and learned has mostly vanished, yet people assume they can do without all of the step-by-step learning of the basics, and without the repetition that took place in a traditional apprenticeship. Apprenticeship seems like a quaint, old-fashioned method for transmitting the craft – something that we could handle more efficiently now. While it is true that there have been huge advances in both the proliferation of information and in some of our tools (mostly machines), both of which make it easier to come by a basic level of competence, this doesn't go very far in making up for a lack of experience. You still have to coordinate your muscles and joints along with your tools to carry out your intentions. This mastery comes only from practice.

It's pretty much a given that most woodworkers don't like the idea of practice. Very few of us will go to the workbench and just make sawcuts for an hour or two to perfect saw technique, or would even think to spend time practicing accurate cuts on the band saw. It's also true that most woodworkers, even intermediates, don't really know what to practice, or even how to practice.

Let's start with the basics. Certain things need to be learned through repetition. Why? It is impossible to absorb and master more than one or two new things at a time. Even fairly simple new tasks require you to both remember and execute things in a precise order or specific relationship to one another. You can't assume you'll be able to do that through sheer will or brain power. There's too much to concentrate on, and we don't learn that way very well. We need a systematic approach to this process, one that adds new elements into the mix slowly. And these have to be added only after mastering the skills that lead up to the new element.

Of course, repetition alone is not the answer. And it can cause as much damage as it does benefit if you're reinforcing and repeating the wrong way to do something.

Experimentation vs. Practice

In order to reap the benefits of repetition, you need to start with a goal of what you're trying to do. This goal, not surprisingly, should be very specific. What are the specifics of successfully mastering the skill you're working on? They should include getting all of the fundamentals right: body position and motion issues; a clear idea of cutting to a line; issues of cut quality or surface results; etc.

Until you have a clear definition of what you need to do, you're just going to be stumbling around blindly, and any work you do is unlikely to lead you toward mastery. With a good concept of success though, you can begin – not practicing, but experimenting.

You need to experience things to be able to understand how the various elements of what you're supposed to do actually feel. And you need to experiment to figure out how to do things the right way. Then you're ready to begin practicing.

Experimentation is the process of attempting to get where you want to go and evaluating your results. You try out different things. No matter how good a description you have of how something is done, it won't convey how it feels, both when you do it wrong, and when you do it right. Throughout this process, you want to be aware of good fundamentals. There may be an unlimited number of ways of getting something done in woodworking, but for the most part, the fundamentals underlying all of them are pretty much the same.

Experimentation is the combination of a clear concept with a good feedback loop. It is finding out exactly what you need to do and what you need to think about to get what you want. It is probably the most important part of developing your technique as you make all of the fine adjustments necessary to improve.

Once you've discovered a successful path to a particular goal you need to reinforce that path with practice. Practice is the repetition of the right way to do something. Or, as the old saying goes, "Practice doesn't make perfect, perfect practice makes perfect."

There's also more to it than that. Because it's impossible to master complex tasks all at once, practice provides a foundation for the added complexity of a task. Having just learned how to saw properly with a handsaw, you'll likely find your newly acquired technique falling apart when you try to saw to a line. You need to back up and reinforce the basic technique more; establish better "muscle memory" for the task. With enough repetition, you don't have to think about that part of what you're doing when you need to concentrate on the next thing. You've created a neural pathway that is strong enough to survive without conscious attention.

You should be aware of this tendency to lose track of your more basic skills as you push forward to new and more complex ones. It is completely natural, and you should expect it.

The other thing that naturally happens as you add new demands and therefore new things to think about, is that tension starts to creep in to your movements. As a general rule, everything will work better without this tension. If you find that you're not relaxed, it's time to back up a little. Break down what you're trying to do into simpler tasks that can be done more easily, and practice them until they are both reliable and relaxed. Then work your way back up by adding in the things that were causing tension. This is fundamental in learning music, but seems pretty radical when applied to woodworking.

The combination of experimentation (trying things out with a good concept and feedback loop) and practice (reinforcing your success with repetition and again, feedback) provides you with a process for continuous improvement – especially if they are both a part of everything that you do. That should be true of any tool or technique, so long as you know the difference between good and bad, and are willing to work toward better and better results.

How to Practice

How might all of this be done in a real-world situation? Let's take the example of sawing to a line, a core skill for cutting dovetails, tenons and other joints. This is based on handsawing skills, with the added element of cutting closely to a line. This is not all that complex a skill, but it still involves a number of things. The basics of hand and body position come first. Make sure you are comfortable with a proper, relaxed grip on the tool, and a good stance with your forearm aligned with the back of the saw and your arm able to move freely past your hip. Then add in the sawing motion itself, working on a smooth, relaxed stroke. Starting the cut can often be a problem so work on doing this (it often helps to think of almost lifting the saw as you begin the cut, and cutting with only the downward weight of the saw rather than pushing down on it). You'll have to experiment with this until it is comfortable and easy. Then you can think about generating the motion from your shoulder, so that all of your motion is straight back and forth, without any side-to-side wiggle.

As this becomes comfortable, it's time to add in some lines, and to see how well you can cut next to them. What adjustments have to be made? A little more pressure to one side or the other? Make your adjustments and then practice some more. Eventually, the goal is to have all of your concentration on technique fade away, leaving you to concentrate strictly on where you're cutting. If you find you don't have a good concept of where to cut, you can even work on this as a separate task. Oddly enough, this can be done at the band saw. That can remove all of the distracting physical work, so you don't need to do anything but think about exactly where you're cutting (which is how it should be once you've practiced enough with your saw).

It's also possible to incorporate some of this experimentation and practice into your projects. For example, if you would like to make a table with cabriole legs, lay out and cut six legs. By the time you get to number six, you'll have a far better idea of what you're doing, and numbers one and two will probably be recognized as the experimental pieces that they were. Cutting a small dovetailed box could be similar project, but don't plan on it being a gift – make it as a box for storing sandpaper, pencils or the like, and don't worry about it. The second or third box will be better. Building this low-stress practice into making an actual piece of furniture is a great way to improve. The practice is not abstract; it matters if the dovetails fit or the legs match. But there's not a whole lot of stress about experimenting or making mistakes.

It's fun to see your progress as you work through these projects. Just don't expect that progress will proceed in a straight line toward excellence. There will always be plateaus and setbacks along the way. Keep an eye on your fundamentals during any of these setbacks.

Practice and experimentation are not limited to hand-tool work. It might seem odd to practice at the table saw or on the jointer, but it's definitely a good idea. Boards of different sizes may call for very different approaches, movements and hand positions. The best approach on either of these tools is to experiment with the machine off. Look for strategies for feeding material smoothly and without hesitation, concentrating on body and foot position, and how you're going to move your hands to get the smoothest feed possible. You'll discover the best way to hold the work, and where and how to push. Then you can reinforce the successful combination of elements with a practice pass or two (with the machine still off). Finally, you can turn on your machine and get to work, concentrating on control, safety and accuracy in your cuts.

Mental Practice

Woodworking isn't only about physical tasks. It's just as important to do mental practice. There are two distinctly different ways to do this. The first of these is the mental rehearsal. This is similar to a ski racer running entirely through a race course in his or her mind. The skier will picture in great detail body position at each moment, and even what he or she needs to concentrate on throughout each turn and change in the terrain throughout the course. This is similar to envisioning the entire process of building your project in advance. If you can build it first in your head (down to the littlest details), you've got a much better chance of doing it in reality. This is just as true of small-scale tasks as well as an on entire project.

The other form of mental practice is improving your concentration. The ability to concentrate well for long stretches of time is one of the biggest differences between pros and amateurs. You can actually practice the ability to maintain focus throughout a cut or a process. The basic idea is to extend a little bit at a time the amount of time you can keep your focus. It helps to have a clear idea of where you're going before you get started, so you don't have to stop to figure out new aspects of the task (and break the focus). In this way, the two types of mental practice are actually related.

Warming Up

You should also be aware of the concept of warming up. This is something that musicians and athletes almost always do.

What is warming up? For athletes, it's both a process of getting the blood flowing and the muscles working at their best, and getting re-acquainted with how various movements feel. The human body is not a machine, and even doing exactly the same thing on different days rarely feels exactly the same. Muscles may be sore or tired, the body may be reacting to cold or heat or illness or even what was just eaten. There are even certain biochemical processes that have to start up in order for you to function at your best. All of this may influence just how your body feels, and you need a little time to adjust for all of these factors. Warming is also the process of getting your feedback loop engaged. It allows for some quick experimentation to rediscover the right way to do what you're trying to do.

Don't just dive right in and start cutting your tenons; do some easy sawing first to get re-acquainted with the saw, get the muscles back in the right groove and focus on how a proper cut feels. You can do the same thing with a hand plane, and use the first few minutes to be sure that the tool is set perfectly as well. It rarely takes more than a minute or two of this, but those few moments will pay off with better results once you get started on the real work.

There is certainly less need to warm up for machine work, although a practice run with the machine off can often expose potential problems and allow you to work out how best to do something.

Strengths and Weaknesses

It's a natural tendency to want to see positive results from your work. This often leads people to work only on the things that they are good at. By all means, work to your strengths. But don't neglect your weaknesses. Your weaknesses provide you with the opportunity to make the biggest improvements to your abilities. And that's where you need the most practice.

It's also worth figuring out why some things are easier for you than others. Is there anything you can do to transfer over your confidence in some things to other areas of your work? Usually, the answer is to practice!

TWELVE

PUTTING IT ALL TOGETHER

Increasing your knowledge of wood, of tools, and of your body should make you a better woodworker. But you'll boost your ability to improve even more by using this knowledge as a foundation. What you build on top of this foundation will determine your further growth. Mastery of the essential knowledge should make it far easier to both understand and assimilate the wealth of information available elsewhere.

This knowledge should make it easier to learn from what you're doing as well. When you understand the fundamental principles and body mechanics behind tool use, and combine that with a clear idea of your end results, teaching yourself becomes as much a part of learning as having someone teach you. The universal nature of these principles means that you'll also have a head start on assimilating new methods and techniques. Even your tools can show you what needs to be done.

Learning From Others

Why should it be easier to learn from someone else now? There are a few reasons. If you're having trouble with any of the fundamentals, working with a good teacher is the best and easiest way to find guidance. He or she will be able to pinpoint problems and offer up possible corrections. Your increased awareness of the importance and relevance of this information should make it easier to incorporate what you've learned.

Another reason to take a class is to learn new techniques. Your understanding of the importance of fundamentals will give you insight into how and why your instructor is doing something a certain way, and not just what they're doing. Watch the instructor to see how he or she builds the process out of fundamentals. There are all kinds of reasons why you might not be able to follow that exact path, but you want to understand the overall structure of what they do.

A good instructor will have figured out methods that will work for a majority of students (and will communicate how and why a technique or approach works). But everyone is different. The methods may not work for you. You can and should make changes and choices based on your own strengths and weaknesses. You may also have preferences for a particular tool or style of working (hand tools only, no hand tools, etc.) that might make a method better or worse for you. In other words, you may have to look further than that instructor's method. Keep in mind that there are countless ways to do almost everything in woodworking. And it doesn't matter one bit which of these you choose, if it gets the job done for you.

Stay open to learning from anything and anyone. Be curious even about the stuff that seems wrong to you. If someone is able to successfully use a technique, it isn't wrong. Just because something seems wrong relative to what you have experienced or have learned (especially in a dogmatic way) before doesn't mean it is wrong. There may even be something in a "wrong way" that you can make use of. But first, you need to understand both how and why it works. What are the reasons behind the technique or approach? Does it pay attention to all of the fundamentals? And how might it be useful to you?

Some of the time, you will find methods that really don't adhere to the fundamentals. You can't get away with ignoring wood behavior, but you actually can get away with poor body mechanics. The human body is almost infinitely adaptable, and with dogged pursuit of a goal, even a "wrong way" might work. It may also lead to carpal tunnel syndrome, a sore back, or worse.

Improving Your Concept

The stronger your concept of exactly what you want to do, the more likely you will be to actually do just that. Improving your concept is not hard, but does take work. And even the easiest steps are often ignored.

Most woodworkers prefer to build from plans. There's nothing inherently limiting in that. But you need to look at plans as a record of how someone else decided to do something, and then fully understand why he or she chose to do it that way. Simply following someone else's instructions usually means you won't understand the reasons behind a particular approach. And that is definitely going to limit you.

Take the time to go through the plans over and over. Find the mistakes that are there – or figure out why you think there's a mistake, and make the corrections you think should be made. Then make up your own cutlist (even if there's one already provided). Your cutlist should be carefully annotated for appropriate wood and joinery choices. You want to understand the project as well as if you had designed it. This is important. If you don't understand the designer's choices, you won't really understand what's going on or why. And you won't be able to make informed choices about following the plans or choosing to make your own modifications.

Most people are not comfortable with this approach to woodworking. It's a far cry from just going down to the shop and building something, at least at first. But it is also much more involving once you get going. You'll have a much clearer idea of what's happening, so you'll work with more focus (which is one of the main pleasures of woodworking no matter how you approach it). You're also much more likely to improve your work. Remember that the more you understand about the destination, the more likely you are to get there – and get there efficiently and accurately.

That brings up another topic: learning more about design. George Walker, the Design Matters columnist for *Popular Woodworking Magazine* wrote, "design is the link in the chain that makes a complete artisan. It unites imagination and skill into something greater, and it takes you places skill alone would never find, and skill spurs imagination to scale heights beyond your present reach."

Design means exploring a whole range of choices – visual and expressive, as well as structural – of how to build something. You don't need to see yourself as especially creative to design something. You do need to be able to come up with and then choose between possible solutions. The more you do this, the more you'll start to see the differences between solutions. This is a great way to improve your "eye" for furniture. And this eye for furniture helps you to refine your goals and dramatically increases your understanding of furniture a little bit at a time.

Learning On Your Own

Learning on your own is a major part of improving. Even working with an instructor full time, it's still your responsibility to assimilate what's being offered. Ultimately, you have to discover how you will best be able to do a particular task. It will help greatly to know how other people do it. But that doesn't tell you how it feels or how to concentrate on the right things. You need courage to experiment, fortitude to practice and dedication to stick with it.

You also need to avoid getting too comfortable. Be eager to challenge yourself a little bit more with each project. Don't just look for projects that are harder, though. Look for things that will also get you excited about your work.

Play around in the shop. Your shop is the ultimate toy room. Try to find the childlike wonder in your work there once in a while. Do things without specific goals – just for fun. Explore.

And practice. Set aside a little time and a bit of inexpensive wood for working on dovetails, or mortise-and-tenon joints, or whatever else needs work. Find a way to make it fun. Make a deal with a friend to each cut a certain number of practice joints, or reward yourself with that new tool you want – but only if you first get your skills up to speed.

When you're learning on your own, you'll need to get good at solving problems. Woodworking is a process of adjusting on the fly to all kinds of dynamic changes. Every board presents its own set of challenges, and you have to adjust to grain-direction changes, dimensional movement and even variable moisture content. Your tools change constantly. A perfectly sharp edge starts to break down as soon as you start to use it, and you have to be aware of that and adjust for it as necessary (as well as determine when you should re-sharpen). Tools also go out of adjustment for various reasons. You might bump a plane or not tighten a screw down tightly enough, allowing something to shift. Something in the wood might dull or nick a blade. Machines suffer from wear and tear on bearings, brushes and belts, and go out of alignment. Bolts may loosen up because of vibration. You'll need to rely on feedback to tell you when things are changing so you can react quickly, but you still need to figure out exactly what's going wrong.

Just because you're paying attention doesn't mean it will be easy to figure out exactly what's happening when something changes or starts to go wrong. This problem is especially acute for the beginner, who is constantly faced with unknowns. Is it me? Is it the tool? Or is it the wood? These are all good questions that everyone has to ask when things go wrong. It's sometimes the case that you just have to make enough mistakes to tell. But regardless of your experience, you've got to figure things out to continue. And only then will the experience be valuable when things go wrong next time.

A Checklist

The best approach to figuring out what's wrong is to make up a mental checklist. Play detective, and run through the list of the usual suspects.

Body mechanics – is it you? Other than taking a lesson, where an instructor might be able to point out problems, you might try taking a quick video of yourself working. This should give you some insight into what you're actually doing. Are you using your body correctly and relying on lower body or bigger muscles for power? Is your body position good? Do you look balanced? How is your alignment?

- Are you working too hard?
- Is the tool sharp? Don't assume that a sharpening will last forever. It's easy enough to check.
- Is the tool set up properly? Questions of tool set-up might include:
- Is the back of your chisel flat? Is your handplane adjusted properly, with the blade square and set to an appropriate depth? Is everything on your handplane tightened down appropriately, or are things loose enough to move or vibrate?

- Are the table saw table (the miter slots) and the table saw fence parallel to the blade? Is the blade actually square to the table? Are the tables on your jointer parallel and set correctly? If the outfeed table isn't aligned perfectly with the height of the cutters, you'll never get a flat edge. Are there nicks in the jointer knives? The little ridges that the nicks leave will cause the wood to ride up on the outfeed table, making it much harder to cut a straight edge.
- Is it the wood? Just because you've flattened a board doesn't mean it will stay flat. Do you need to compensate for changes in grain direction? If you can't change the direction of the cut, can you use a steeper cutting angle, or switch to a scraper? It might even be how you're holding the work on your workbench. Clamp something too tightly between dogs and you might spring the board out of flat. Any sag in your tail vise might have a similar effect.

All of these questions (and more) should lead you toward a solution of the problem. And each time you go through this process, it should get easier. These problems aren't even really mistakes; they are just the reality of working with wood. But they are just as important as mistakes to your learning and improvement. They build up a framework of solutions to the problems you'll face every day in the shop.

Not only do you need to add woodworking information to this framework of essential information, you want to also bring in experiences from other endeavors and successes. This synthesis is how you can come up with solutions that work the best for you.

Learning From Your Tools

In the conclusion of his book *The New Traditional Woodworker*, Jim Tolpin writes, "The more I work by hand, the more I learn; I find the tools themselves teach me how to use them in the most effective way." This is certainly the case. But it's only true under certain conditions. You need to know what you're trying to do with the tools. And you need to understand the fundamentals of the wood, how the tools should work and how your body needs to work. Put all of that together with some experimentation, and good tools really can teach you what to do.

There's much more to learn about every one of the topics in this book. Woodworking is phenomenally rich in methods, techniques and creative possibilities. Let this book be the foundation upon which you build – the framework into which you can fit more of the details. There are plenty of other opinions, and countless methods for doing just about anything. Seek out this information, and learn what you can from it. But most of all, get to work, and get as much done as you can, so you can learn, experiment and enjoy your woodworking as much as possible.

AFTERWORD

There are countless ways to do almost everything in woodworking. But in truth, the only valid way to decide if a method is good or not is to examine the results. To put it simply, if it works, it's not broken. There are no style points granted for good body position while working on cutting a set of dovetails.

How do I balance that statement against a whole book's worth of telling you the best way to improve your woodworking? I have found that certain ways work better than others, and there are plenty of solid reasons why they work better. But I'm not saying that these methods need to be followed slavishly, or (double negative alert) that not working this way is necessarily wrong. Or at least not if you're getting great results.

If what you're doing works, then it probably isn't wrong. There are two reasons that I need to qualify that statement with a "probably." First, there are some safety issues that might make a particular approach most definitely wrong. The safe way is always preferable. And second, you might be putting your body under undue stress while working in a less efficient manner. If you're doing a lot of this, you may be at risk for repetitive motion injuries.

If, on the other hand, you're having trouble getting the results you would like in your woodworking, than these suggestions may help you to find your way.

What I've described throughout this book is a combination of practical knowledge and applied knowledge. You can learn to understand the wood by reading about wood's structure, although you'll need to experience countless examples of different properties and problems to start to achieve mastery. But no amount of reading will allow you to conquer the various movements needed to plane a board effectively, or to saw a dovetail. You certainly need to figure out what to do (and the book should help with that), but then you need to learn how to do it by repeating the new skill, experiencing it over and over, making the various mistakes that will inevitably come and learning the intricacies and quirks of doing it in a variety of woods. And then you need to practice some more. You can't learn how to ride a bicycle by reading about it, and you can't learn how to saw tenons just by reading about it either. The complexity of the task is just too great. And understanding that complex tasks can't be learned by osmosis is important to having the patience to persevere.

There are many terrific resources that can provide you with much more detailed information about any of the topics in this book. This is a small selection of the books that can add significantly to your stores of knowledge.

- *The Perfect Edge: The Ultimate Guide to Sharpening for Woodworkers*, Ron Hock, Popular Woodworking Books, 2009

- *Taunton's Complete Illustrated Guide to Sharpening*, Thomas Lie-Nielsen, Taunton Press, 2004

- *Understanding Wood: A Craftsman's Guide to Wood Technology*, R. Bruce Hoadley, Taunton Press, 2000

- *Handplane Essentials*, Christopher Schwarz, Popular Woodworking Books, 2009

- *The Handplane Book*, Garrett Hack, Taunton Press, 1999

- *Band Saw Handbook*, Mark Duginske, Sterling Publishing Company, 1989

- *The Table Saw Book*, Kelly Mehler, Taunton Press, 2003

Dedication
To Becky, Isaac and Ariel

Acknowledgements
It's surprising how many people have to put up with you while you're writing a book, and just how much they have to put up with. A big thanks to everyone who listened patiently (or at least pretended very well) as I explored and tested out my ideas, especially Chris Schwarz, Megan Fitzpatrick, Jameel Abraham, Deneb Puchalski, Marc Adams, Andy Brownell, and especially my wife, Becky, and my daughter, Ariel.

Additional thanks to Chris and Megan for their critical input and review. Chris also helped get this all moving from an exciting idea to a real book.

And great thanks to David Thiel for ushering the idea through the process of turning it all into a book. This book couldn't have happened without his patience, guidance and skill.

And a special thanks to all of my students, who for years have been trusting me to teach them what to do, little realizing how much they were actually teaching me.

Distributed in Canada by Fraser Direct
100 Armstrong Avenue
Georgetown, Ontario L7G 5S4
Canada

Distributed in the U.K. and Europe by
F&W Media International, LTD
Brunel House, Ford Close
Newton Abbot
TQ12 4PU, UK
Tel: (+44) 1626 323200
Fax: (+44) 1626 323319
E-mail: enquiries@fwmedia.com

Distributed in Australia by Capricorn Link
P.O. Box 704
Windsor, NSW 2756
Australia

Visit our website at popularwoodworking.com or
our consumer website at shopwoodworking.com for
more woodworking information projects.

Other fine Popular Woodworking Books are available from your local bookstore or direct from the
publisher.

16   15   14   13   12   5   4   3   2   1

Acquisitions editor: David Thiel
Designer: Elyse Schwanke
Production coordinator: Mark Griffin

ABOUT THE AUTHOR

Jeff Miller is a designer, craftsman, prolific writer and an
active teacher both at his own woodworking school
in Chicago, and at furniture schools around the country.
His furniture has won numerous awards, has been in shows
around the country, and is in the collection of the Chicago
History Museum. His book *Chairmaking & Design* won the
Stanley Award for Best How-To Book of 1997 (and
his companion video *Chairmaking Techniques* won best
video as well). He has also written the books *Beds* and
Children's Furniture Projects, and has contributed chapters
to *Furniture for All Around the House* and *Storage
Projects for All Around the House,* for The Taunton Press,
and is a frequent contributor to *Fine Woodworking* and
Popular Woodworking Magazine.

Metric Conversion Chart

TO CONVERT	TO	MULTIPLY BY
Inches	Centimeters	2.54
Centimeters	Inches	0.4
Feet	Centimeters	30.5
Centimeters	Feet	0.03
Yards	Meters	0.9
Meters	Yards	1.1

Read This Important Safety Notice

To prevent accidents, keep safety in mind while you work.
Use the safety guards installed on power equipment; they are
for your protection.

When working on power equipment, keep fingers away
from saw blades, wear safety goggles to prevent injuries from
flying wood chips and sawdust, wear hearing protection and
consider installing a dust vacuum to reduce the amount of
airborne sawdust in your woodshop.

Don't wear loose clothing, such as neckties or shirts with
loose sleeves, or jewelry, such as rings, necklaces or bracelets,
when working on power equipment. Tie back long hair to
prevent it from getting caught in your equipment.

People who are sensitive to certain chemicals should check
the chemical content of any product before using it.

Due to the variability of local conditions, construction
materials, skill levels, etc., neither the author nor Popular
Woodworking Books assumes any responsibility for any
accidents, injuries, damages or other losses incurred resulting
from the material presented in this book.

The authors and editors who compiled this book have
tried to make the contents as accurate and correct as
possible. Plans, illustrations, photographs and text have been
carefully checked. All instructions, plans and projects should
be carefully read, studied and understood before beginning
construction.

Prices listed for supplies and equipment were current at
the time of publication and are subject to change.

INDEX

IDEAS. INSTRUCTION. INSPIRATION.

These and other great Popular Woodworking products are available at your local bookstore, woodworking store or online supplier.

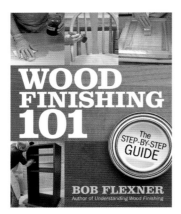

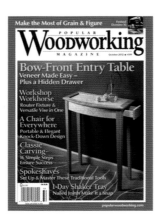

WOOD FINISHING 101
By Bob Flexner
Wood finishing doesn't have to be complicated or confusing. *Wood Finishing 101* boils it down to simple step-by-step instructions and pictures on how to finish common woods using widely available finishing materials. Bob Flexner has been writing about and teaching wood finishing for more than 20 years.

paperback • 128 pages

WEEKEND WOODWORKER'S PROJECT COLLECTION
This book has 40 projects from which to choose and, depending on the level of your woodworking skills, any of them can be completed in one or two weekends. Project s include: a game box, jewelry box, several styles of bookcases and shelves, mirrors, picture frames and more.

paperback • 256 pages

POPULAR WOODWORKING MAGAZINE
Whether learning a new hobby or perfecting your craft, *Popular Woodworking Magazine* provides seven issues a year with the expert information you need to learn the skills, not just build the project. Find the latest issue on newsstands, or you can order online at popularwoodworking.com.

SHOPCLASS VIDEOS
From drafting, to dovetails and even how to carve a ball-and-claw foot, our ShopClass Videos let you see the lesson as if you were standing right there.

Available at shopwoodworking.com
DVD & Instant download

POPULAR WOODWORKING'S VIP PROGRAM
Get the Most Out of Woodworking!

Join the ShopWoodworking VIP program today for the tools you need to advance your woodworking abilities. Your one-year paid renewal membership includes:

• *Popular Woodworking Magazine* (1 year/7 issue U.S. subscription — a $21.97 value)

• *Popular Woodworking Magazine* CD — Get all issues of *Popular Woodworking Magazine* from 2006 to to 2010 (a $64.95 value!)

• *The Best of Shops & Workbenches* CD — 62 articles on workbenches, shop furniture, shop organization and essential jigs and fixtures (a $15 value)

• Roubo Plate 11 Poster — A beautiful 18" x 24" reproduction of Plate 11 from Andre Roubo's 18th-century masterpiece *L'Art du Menuisier,* on heavy, cream-colored stock

• 20% Members-Only Savings on 6-Month Subscription for ShopClass OnDemand

• 10% Members-Only Savings at Shopwoodworking.com

• 10% Members-Only Savings on FULL PRICE Registration for Woodworking In America Conference (Does Not Apply with Early Bird Price)

• and more....

Visit **popularwoodworking.com** to see more woodworking information by the experts, learn about our digital subscription and sign up to receive our weekly newsletter at popularwoodworking.com/newsletters/

    FOLLOW POPULAR WOODWORKING